Bedtime Stories For Kids Daily Challenge: Daily Sleep Stories & Guided Meditation To Help Toddlers & Kids Fall Asleep Fast, Develop Mindfulness, Bond With Parents & Relax Deeply

By Mindfulness Meditations Made Easy

© **Copyright 2020 - All rights reserved.**

The content contained within this book may not be reproduced, duplicated or transmitted without direct written permission from the author or the publisher.

Under no circumstances will any blame or legal responsibility be held against the publisher, or author, for any damages, reparation, or monetary loss due to the information contained within this book; either directly or indirectly.

Legal Notice:

This book is copyright protected. This book is only for personal use. You cannot amend, distribute, sell, use, quote or paraphrase any part, or the content within this book, without the consent of the author or publisher.

Disclaimer Notice:

Please note the information contained within this document is for educational and entertainment purposes only. All effort has been executed to present accurate, up to date, and reliable, complete information. No warranties of any kind are declared or implied. Readers acknowledge that the author is not engaging in the rendering of legal, financial, medical or professional advice.

Contents

Nature Stories 1

Animal Stories 11

Barn Story 21

Protection Story 29

Flower Story 40

Security Story 50

Tree story 61

Trust Story 70

Water Fountain story 80

Creativity Story 90

River Story 99

Friendship Story 108

Mermaid story 118

Sea Travel Story 128

Whale Story 137

Dolphin story 147

Underwater Story 156

Rainbow story 166

Parents Story 176

Turtle Story 185

Long life story 195

Fire Story 205

Salamander Story 214
Jungle story 224
Monkey story 235
Rescue story 249
Bird story 252
Prince and Princess story 256
Fairytale story 261

Nature Stories

<u>1378 words, 20 minutes</u>

Once upon a time in a mystical land there lived a renowned Mother, Mataja, who was the keeper of the land and holder of the keys to the sacred castles. She grew up on this land under a tree and she lived out in Nature the whole day and night. Her wonderful long hair in silver shone with experience and she was very wise.
Mataja could speak to the flowers and to the animals in respect and tolerance all the beings helped her and the people of this land.
When Mataja was outdoors, she collected herbs for medicine to bring this medicine to the needy. She was knowledgeable of all the flowers and trees, bees, animals and all you can know about nature.
When one was pregnant she knew exactly what to do, and which foods to

supply as well as how the child would be delivered.

In the realms there also lived a king who was desiring a son, but He and His Queen were not able, until Mataja organized a walk in the forest with the king, to find the certain remedy for relief.

We can imagine a wild and lush forest that holds many green leaves, colourful fruits and flowers. The path into the forest is only accessible with the help of Mataja, who guides the King into the forest.

The flowers are greeting you, she smiles and gently stops, lets give these flowers attention and smile back. Smile. The flowers sense the attention and are happy that you are visiting.

The wonderful flowers in this mystical forest smell, and soothing scent arises at the tip of our nose. Inhale and Exhale, it is the best medicine. Where we start our life is with a simple breath. Flowers

and other beings do the same. They all are breathing.
Breathing is the best and essential medicine. This is why this forest is sacred, because it breathes like we do.

Let's sit here and I think we have almost found what we are looking for. Mataja prepares a space for the King.
Meditate and I will be back with a handful of ingredients.
Then we start a fire to heat the water and to make tea. The sacred tea with the healing flowers will aid you.
Just sit here and feel at home, relax and be comfortable. Meditate and Breathe.

The King relaxes and feels pleasant in this Nature. Finally someone is taking care, he thinks. Suddenly, the trees bow to the king and start to talk: Welcome dear King, we are the mystical forest and here to greet you.

The king awakes from his meditation and gently smiles. I am happy to have you here and help me, we really want a son, and the queen is ready to receive one.

Mataja comes back with the basket full of herbs and flowers - she smiles, too, I am glad the forest welcomes you and bows. We are now ready to return to the Palast and bring the herbs to the Queen.

On a beautiful alley way the king looks into sky and wonders what the stars are saying, there must be a special occasion be happening in the heavens.

Mataja smiles and tells that every occassion is special, every being is one of a kind, and every single breath is unique.
Mataja, you are very wise and know Nature so well.

Nature is happy with me, because I am happy in nature. Lets bring these to the Queen and help her for her birth.
While the King and Mataja are on the Way home, the Queen is in her day

dream and suddenly a white tiger comes into her dreams.

The Tiger announces, a Son will be born to you very soon, wait, be patient and constantly trust your kingdom.
The Queen is in wonder and startled looks outside the window. There the King and Mataja approach the Kingdom. Trust.

Trust me, bring these herbs to the Queen and let her bathe in the flowers. When you are ready, come outside for a small walk to the fire place, where I will be preparing the tea.
Mataja holds up the herbs and flowers for the kingdom and the Son shall be born.

As they bathe and wait, as the Nature is kind, so mercyful with a peaceful state of mind, the wonderful story will unwind, unfold and gracefully like the Queen bathing in flowers, dressed in garments of purity, the King and Queen shall be in Unity.

The Birds and Bees sing and hum, the echo of the flowers and trees enlightens the whole forest kingdom and beyond, the villages and towns, they All hear, a Son is born, a Son is born.
With flutes and harps, trumpets and drums, the festivity goes 9 months long. Everyday they do the best for the Queen, serving her flowers and tea.

Once the Queen is happy, the kingdom will live in harmony.
So together they on the fire place, sharing a cup of unity.
Peace be with the forest, happiness be with the water, all come together at open fire, under the same sky.

The stars are out and shine oh so bright. There also moon reflecting this light. The fire burns and illuminates the happy faces of the party that celebrates with joy and dance.

The Nature is all happy too, as it watches us, the Happiness of us is also the happiness of All, Mataja says wisely. Let's prepare the blessing.

The oldest of the trees so wise and tall, old as no one ever could count, is now in presence to bestow a blessing for safety and security.

Everyone in the party is quiet and you can only hear the wind whistling in the dancing leaves of the tree, Maramta, the old and wise tree still wears fruit and shakes one of his branches.

With these fruits you shall feed your Son, so he might become a good heir with strength, beauty and grace he shall grow to be a wise man, Maramba smiles as gently as a tree can smile.

Beautiful world of speaking and smiling trees,
All happens under the night skies harmonies,
All is arranged in an order, with beauty and grace,

We look into the Moments space, there's a gentle face.
We find space, to take a deep breath and rest -
Let's wait for the best -
The blessing of the tree, the music to be free,
The dance, the music, the night liberate thee.

Mataja and Maramba bow in dignity and peace. The party is dissolved into eternity, the Waiting for the New born begins, and all prepare with joy and happiness. The Vision of the Queen became true, and the Son is born. With tender skin and lotus eyes, that shine like the sun, the baby is named, Samatura, the one that is always in balance and peace.

The Kingdom cheerful decorates everything in bright colours and the garden of the king is open for everyone to see, the first steps of a toddler, in grace and dignity.

Even sometimes when we fall, there is always the help of someone. Mother Nature holds us on this earth and blesses us with light and love. The trees provide the shadow, the water brings purity, fire light and in the night there the stars shine.

Imagine this world is all in the air, a possibility for everyone. As we are children of this earth, the presence under the sun, breathing the same air we are all in care. Nature is so rich and kind, everyone can find, a throne of the self. The body is here to help. Bringing us from one place to another, your hands, legs, head and heart all here for a reason.

Let's find the treasure of Joy that is in Nature, always and ever. Say Hello to the trees and smile. Be happy, that one is here.
Breathe and relax, all is friendly, as we are a friend to the earth, the Kingdom of Trees, Animals, Humans alike.

So we can imagine walking in the garden of the kingdom, together with the Son, the King and Queen, because we are all just a big family. See yourself happy and be happy, one is alive.
Smile, relax and have a good night.

Animal Stories

<u>1564 words, 25 minutes</u>

There once lived two monkeys in this mystical forest, Ernst and Herbert were very unusually clever and so smart, they went to the best universities, even sometimes people wonder how is this possible?

These monkeys had a teacher, a wise turtle named Kurma. This turtle lived just close to the mystical forest on the sea and hence the turtle holds time and space upwards, it just watches and observes the coming and going of the people. Kurma knows every little detail and habit, even someone scratching ones head out of uncertainty. The turtle observes the Nature all around and hence is very watchful and wise.

As the Monkey, Herbert and Ernst were playing, they wanted to show how clever they are and tried to play a game with the turtle. It is a musical game, where one is taking over the sound of the other one and adding more sounds to the circle. This game the two monkeys practice while the turtle played once and made so many sounds at the same moment, the monkeys were so in awe, they fell out of their rhythm and asked for guidance: How can you do so many things at once, just please accept us, and maybe you wise turtle can show us how you do the sounds of many ways.

Many ways I have travelled, Kurma says, across the land and see, long journeys come to ease, when I look these, you two are welcome and accepted, I may show you how.
So day and night the monkey sit besides the turtle and study with Kurma.

Sometimes, like us, they were just sitting in peace, just breathing and having a meditation.

Kurma guides this meditation and says, this meditation will bring harmony and well-being to your body and to your mind, that sits inside every cell of your body. Your body is made up of trillions of cells and every cell is alive and breathes.

Here, we can make all the body breathe, together, in and out, gently and slow, think about me, I am wise, gentle and so slow. Breathe in and out, gentle and slow.

Do you feel the relief and the calmness and peace?

Breathing into the nose, and breathing out of the nose, you can rest your eyes, half open, half closed. This will help to elevate any stress or disease, within the matter of a breath, there is the whole universe coming in and going out.

The breathing comes and goes, in and out, equally in and out, equally in and equally out again. Do you feel it?
Now focus on the nose-tip, and watch it, like opening of a river, the air streams in

and out, it travels along your nose-tip, into the nose and to the heart.

Feel the rhythm of the heart, do you feel? Feel the breathing streaming into the lungs and around the heart there is a feeling. Whatever this feeling may be, you are alive, breathing, and shall be happy. Be happy and content. Let the breathing move naturally and come to ease.

In the whole wide animal world I have met many teachers, but the real teacher sits within your heart. From your heart this inner teacher guides everything that is around you. Try to find this inner teacher within your heart. Breathe naturally and come to ease.

Once, Kurma explains to the monkeys, once I was meditating in the vast ocean and I noticed, no I need a good and calm place, then I meditated on the still lake and I noticed, no this lake is still but I can do better, and then I meditated upon a mountain. The monkeys look at each other, how can you walk upon a mountain?

The turtle Kurma smiles and says, easily I have found a guide, that carries me up there, so I asked the Eagle, please can you help me to the peak of this mountain? Of course, the eagle wanted to have me as lunch, but I offered my service, life-long, I shall bring you fresh sea fruits just let me be on this mountain for once.

In a lifetime of a turtle, Kurma laughs, who has thought to be on a mountain peak? Eventually the Eagle and I became friends and Elly the Eagle is also bringing me back down again. This is important, because sometimes I totally fall into deep meditation. It is almost like sleep, but I can move in my mind, which is the imagination to be wherever and whatever you like.

However, Elly did not forget me, and I am always thankful for her upliftment and for the chance to fly with an eagle once. Do you like to come on a flight or do you like to stay on your trees?

The monkeys look at each other, always together, now they were sure, only one can fly to the mountain with the eagle. But how can the monkeys know who is the one that can go on the adventure. Maybe Kurma knows a way to find the chosen one.

Kurma smiles, as I see it, you are both ready, but one is more ready than the other, find out who it is by finding Elly, who ever finds the eagle might go to the mountain peak with her.

The monkey start to seek out in the forest for the eagle, as one climbs up the tree, the other is sure, maybe I can make it onto the top alone. Without a word, both search the way, one calling from a tree, and the other one straight forward to the top.

There once were to monkeys, longing to go to the mountain peak, but only the

way was clear from the birds eye and beak,
The sound of an Eagle echoes in the air, oh where oh where, I come to be named, Elly the Eagle world-renowed and famed, as I am not hungry for turtles, making Kurma my friend, he probably has some time to spend.

So Elly lands on the shore of the ocean to find Kurma who tells her about the two monkeys looking for a way to get to the top. The Eagle is laughing and finds that a monkeys belongs to the trees, but somewhere he sees, a monkey, on the way to the top.
Eagle Eyes so sharp see a monkey very smart, climbing with the help of a Yak, who knows the mountains without stop. They start to witness the other monkey calling from the tree, please dear Eagle help me!

The Turtle says, go before he starts to lose, let all be winners, and leave me behind. The story is here to unwind, as the Eagle flies to pick up Ernst from the tree, carrying him to the Peak. Herbert on the Yak, named Wadu, come with a scream WUHU! By the moment Herbert gets of the Yak to find a stand he mets the moment exactly where Ernst is here to land. Both monkeys on the peak, with the help of a friend, this has long no end, because the competition is off, as all realize where they are.

With a wonderful view, the panorama unfolds,
It is a blessed scene, one that Nature upholds.
The beauty of the moment, the wide horizon
And before, the golden sun.

Setting into the ocean, all realize, there is just one watching them all, Kurma, the turtle.
Laughing and laughing Kurma's laugh echoes to the peak - they all did it with grace and ease, one on a Yak, one with an Eagle, coming together, landing on the spot.

A while it takes, all look at each other, until Kurma calls; It's ok, you all are Winners! Come down and let's celebrate.
The Yak, The Eagle and the two monkeys choose the easy way down, to meet and party on the sunset beach.

Beautiful waves of bliss, and sunset stunning as always, the animals party a safe coming home. The night is there and the sky turns into beautiful rose, purple and blue, may this party be also one for you?
Together we sit and breathe, we celebrate life as it is. Together we almost reached the sky, but only now I wonder why.
Kurma helps us to see, everything is a possibility.
Maybe alone we are not strong, but together -
we can sing a harmonious song.

In harmony, one can be brave enough to have a friend, to take the chance and ask for help, may I have a hand?

At the moment you land, all is here to understand.
We are alive, thanks to the light, to the sky and the stars that shine oh so bright.

Let's rest and have a good, good night- Kurma holds the attention high; do you know what helps going to sleep? A good night story, but first we relax the body and mind. Slowly, breathe and gentle feel the air stream along the nose to your heart.

Blessed all beings be, and now let's have a Rest In Peace and harmony. Good night and maybe on another note I tell a story of a Yak, an Eagle and two monkeys climbing a rock.

All laugh and happily go for a good nights rest, so we All are a story, at ones best.

Sleep well.

Barn Story

<u>1283 words, 20 minutes</u>

Once there was a beautiful land rich in golden grains and fruits, all coming from the earth. The grass is fresh and green and the field forms around a river stream that provides the land with enough water flow. The farmer there is the One to know, and his name is Rich, like the land is rich, his name is too.
Rich knows everything about the land and he makes his barn open for everyone to visit. He believes in the everyone-is-welcome spirit.

Often there come volunteers to help and learn something that almost is forgotten; the art of making golden bread, from the seed to the bread, one who is ready can see the whole process. Rich is always enthusiastic about this bread and he also says, his bread is like medicine, once you have tasted this bread, you shall go well to bed. It's a bed bread - made from golden flour and fruits, lovely heated over the fire, crusty and crispy, well-done it can last for years and years to come, but the recipe comes from his Father. Richie Rich, his Father was a farmer, too but he was an expert for the Pie. Fruits for the pie, I still wonder why, he never got to be a millionaire, because his Pie is famous around the world. He would only care for the health of the family and the farm.

So, now we can make a journey on the barn, and what else is there to see? Yes, there is a whole cow family! We come along and Mooo, the cows awake, so lovely and kind, giving milk of all kind, sometimes we forget, the milk that is the best for bed.
The best its warm, and a little sweet, like this story. So no worry, all the animals are very well raised, as they have enough to do, Rich gives us a tour.

Here, he says, you can see the most wonderful indigenous cows, which are shy and serene, they love the golden hey and green field. Lets bring them out to the meadow, into the nature, into the grass. Every Cow has a name, Mula, Swaya, Mani, Ana, Vishu, Anja, Sahasra and they all hear very well.

When you call them, they hear you very attentively and Rich knows why. Cows all have a connection to the Milky Way, so all the sounds resonate in Harmony. This is Space-Cow science and I am actually training them to be the first cows in space.
There is always astonishment in a cows face. When you look at them it is definitely wonderful to see a cow in space, but the training is more than an extraordinary phase. Sometimes Rich lets the Cows walk on cushions and feathers, so they prepare for anti-gravity.

In the summer time he lets them wear sun-glasses, cool cows, just to prepare. Of course one makes milk, Rich thinks about the first Space-Milk, but anyhow, the world isn't ready yet, but before we go to bed, a nice warm milk will make us fed, Rich smiles and shows us around the Barn to see the Pigs.

How does a pig make? Yes, this sound is unique as one knows pigs are the best at playing the nose trumpet. Actually Rich is conducting a symphony with the grunts and the moos. Moo Moo here, Grunt Grunt there. A barn is full and everywhere, you see a pig, you see a cow - oh WOW. There is a symphony.

The more we are on the land, the more the fresh air is here to tend. We breathe in and out, gentle and soft the fresh air streams along the nose, around the face and brings us new hope and space. We inhale and exhale, equally in and out again. The barn is still in peace and harmony, and we found a place in-midst the green field, watching the river stream, oh what a wonderful dream, of peace and serenity. There come 5 Chicken and one rooster to call for the evening. It is around that time, the chicken know and the rooster releases a loud: KIKERIKIII, strong and fierce all the chicken cackle and grin, with a victorious win, the farmer Rich starts to spin the weather rose, all animals must go, safe and sound to bed. First the Cows, blankets on top, with a warm and sweet good night, we say good night to all the cows: Good night Mula, good night Sways, good night Mani, Good night Ana, Good night Vishu, good night Anja, good nigh Sahasra, then we say good night to the Pigs, good night Pigs, then we say good night to the chickens and rooster, good night chicken and rooster.

All the beautiful animals live here rich in everyrhing, rich in space and good nights. The more we spend time on the barn, the more we notice the fresh air and calm peaceful evenings. Lets embrace once more, that we have a little oasis of serenity here with us. Lets give Rich and his Father a warm appreciative THANK YOU, lets say it innerly and bring our lips to smile. Lets smile and yawn, smile and relax. Just smile for awhile.

One can always come back to this barn, as this barn is within our heart and we can come here whenever we want. Is there a chance we can play with the cows or watch the pigs, or listen to the barn symphony with all the players, and when it is time, the rooster will let us know.

Now, let's relax the body, from head to toe, and find a comfortable position to rest. Imagine you sink into nice, comfortable hey, very dry and soft. See yourself resting, and feel how your head is relaxed. The forehead is eased and every tissue of your neck and shoulder is relaxed. The arms and hands are relaxing and comfortable. We breathe and feel the relaxation spreading from the heart, to the belly and to the whole back. The whole upper body is relaxed and we breathe, equally in and equally out. We breathe and our thighs, legs, knees, ankles and feet relax, too. All our lower body is relaxed and light. The whole body is becoming lighter and lighter, with every breath we take, the body becomes lighter and lighter. There is more space and we feel the ease in the spine and every cell of the body. We can imagine how beautiful golden light spreads from the heart and and into every cell in the body. Golden light protects us and lets us feel warm and comfortable. The golden is soothing warm, nice and soothing. Every cell of the body is now in harmony and secure, fresh air is streaming into the nostrils and we are aware of the breath. Once more we give thanks to the Mother Land, to the Waters, the Sun and Moon, as well as all the beings.

A golden light expands now from our heart into the world and surrounds the whole world with a beautiful golden light of compassion and safety. We are happy and connected with all the beings. All beings are happy and safe, All beings are happy and safe, All beings are happy and safe.

Let the breathing air flow naturally and gently close your eyes and rest with compassion and kindness for all the beings.

May All beings be Happy and Safe,

May All beings be Happy and Safe,
May All beings be Happy and Safe.

Have a good rest and a soothing night, and if not, just imagine Cows flying in space towards the Milky Way.

Protection Story

<u>1636 words, 25 minutes</u>

Imagine there is a light, a beautiful light, that shines from within your heart. It is so bright and beautiful, it's around your whole body.

Breathe and feel the lightness throughout the whole body. See that light expanding with every breath. In and out, the breathing is equal and natural, the light expands and surrounds even the aura around you.

From within your heart there shines the source of this light and with every breath we illuminate our whole body, from the head, one can see the head glowing in a beautiful protective light, to the feet. With every breath the light travels throughout the body.

We start from the crown of our head, there is a the light slowly sinking into the face. We breathe and with every breath, the light sinks lower and lower into area of the eyes. Our eyes and all the muscles around the eyes are illuminated with protective, healing light.

Just focus on the breathing and let the light sink into the ears, the cheeks and jaw. All the little tissues and membranes are equally illuminated, around the nose, on the jaw, and inside off the head, where the nose meets the mouth. We focus on this point, where the nose meets the mouth and clearly sense our breathing. We can even hear the breath coming in and going out again. It is a constant stream of energy that comes with the air, and the sound is clear and soothing.

One can find comfort in the sound of the breath and know there is a light, a life protection from within and around us.

The Life Breath is everyones mandatory need.and we can connect with this friend our whole life. It is always there for us. Lets breathe again and feel how mandatory and friendly the life air is.

See the focus where the nose and mouth meet.and sense the air coming into the nostrils and going out again. It is a constant Hello, Breath. Goodbye Breath. Always and ever coming and going. We are just witnessing this process, this endless stream and ensure everything is smooth and equal.

Equally in and out again, the protective light shines within our whole head and a feeling of peace and protection spreads around the face. We can smile and ease into the breath. Maybe sigh or yawn, whatever feels now fine with you.

Also note any sensation, whatever it is, warmth, cold, vibrating, tickling, throbbing, pulsing, any sensation is possible, and whatever comes, we keep on breathing.

We see the breath traveling into our nostrils and down the throat into the lungs. From our head and our heart the protective light also illuminates the throat and neck area. Along the spine the protective light shines in every cell from the head, to the throat, to the middle of the body.

Here the light sinks further down with the breath and we include as many parts as possible, like the shoulders and arms, elbows, wrists and hands. All are surrounded with protective light. We can open our hands to the sky and see how the light illuminates now every cell, even the finger tips.

Lets put our hands into our middle, onto the belly and feel into the body. Protective light is spreading from the hands and from the heart into the belly and around the whole lower body. The healing light of protection axpands and brings peace and ease.

We breathe and with every breath the light sinks further down the spine, from the belly to the hips, into the root of the spine. Here we relax and find that the healing light of protection is welcome to also illuminate our thighs, knees, legs, ankles and feet. The healing light of protection even shines into the smallest parts of the tippy toes and brings peace and relaxation.

From the tippy toes we can come upwards, according to our breath we can travel with the awareness, the light of protection up the legs, to the bottom of the spine and again, slowly up the spine to the heart. Here, in the heart we hold this healing light of protection and let it blossom like a flower.

With every breath, each and every pedal of this wonderful flower of light expands from the heart and shines throughout the whole body. The whole flower of light is now really beautiful and blossomed. We can imagine we are meeting a friend, and we can bring this flower as a present to the heart of this friend.

Let's smile and innerly say: Here, this is the light of my heart, may it protect and bring you peace.
You can repeat this prayer and see your friend kindly accepting it.

Here, this is the flower of my heart, may it protect and bring you peace.
Here, this is the flower of my heart, may it protect and bring you peace.
Here, this is the flower of my heart, may it protect and bring you peace.

By saying this we give meaning to the flower and to the light, therefore one knows what this light intends to do.
Protection and Peace is now upon us and we can see the whole body of ours and our friend be illuminated.

By breathing we uphold the light, by breathing we maintain the luminosity.

Whenever we are in a hurry, we can also call this protective light and ask for healing light of protection. Please Light,

Protect me, and give me shelter of Peace.
The healing light is like the breathing always with us, when we are aware of it, it comes into presence.

In our imagination lets wander around our home and in the garden to maintain this healing light. Just breathe and feel the connection to the sunlight. See how the light of protection and the sun light are one and the same.

See the trees and the grass, and know all this is grown from the sunlight, one with the light of protection. See the sky and the endless horizon and know, your inner voice can always call for the light of protection.

May All beings be in protection and Peace,
May All find relaxation and ease.
May All have a life of light and love.
May All live in Peace and Harmony,
May All join the Unity.

For a good nights sleep this protective light can bring us from the unsafe shores of darkness to the beautiful shores of the light kingdom.

Find yourself comfortable and relaxed, you are now safe and in protection. We are sailing over the ocean of darkness, but without any fear, we have friends, teachers, and guides of light on our side.

They know how to steer the ship into the waves, sailing with the wind, even the mermaids are helping us for good fortune and protection. Even the Fish and the Turtles are helping us for good. Also the wind and water, are good to us, soothing when there is too much going on, and there is the sun for direction, in which way to go.

We are in midst the sea, and the elements, as well as all the passengers are chanting a song of protection and good will.

Let's all trust on the travel,

Across the land and sea,
Lets unite people and everyone in balance and harmony.

Look, there might be a long way in front of us,
All we essentially need to do, is to trust & Breathe.
Let's See, together we may live in Harmony.

When there comes a time of sorrow,
We may speak it out and ask: What is going on?
Let's come to shore and find a place of Harmony.

Let's imagine the vessel finds a land, taking on the ropes to the harbour and taking care of all the passengers including one Self. We are safe to shore guided over the sea of ignorance, into the land we finally find peace, protection and harmony.

Let's see and imagine, all there is. The people are smiling and inviting us to come along. Let's celebrate the arrival and say good bye to the day. As the vessel takes off into the sunset, it slowly gets cooler and find a cozy place for the night, are we alright?

Still breathing, into the nostrils and into the heart, the protective light of healing and harmony is illuminating our whole being and we find shelter, with our friends and family.

Let's sing and dance together for good joy and celebration to be healthy and well. Let's chant a simple Mantra for Guidance and Protection of the whole world.

I am the light of the world,
I am the light of the world,
I am, I am, I am the light of the world.

You are the light of the world,
You are the light of the world,
You are, You are, You are the Light of the world.

We are the light of the world,
We are the light of the World,
We are, We are, We are the light of the world.

The sing-song enchants and brings light to the moment, even going to bed, we can shine our light to be safe and sound. Feel the breathing slowly relaxing and smoothly coming in and going out. Let's once more give thanks to the Light, the sun and moon, as well as all the people that shine their light of attention to Us.

Let's gently close our eyes and find our inner paradise, on the safe shores of protection and harmony.
Let's smile and be happy,
Have a deep breath and let yourself sink into the night,
may there always be protection and light.
Have a good, good night.
May there always be light.

Flower Story

<u>1413 words - 20 minutes</u>

Once upon time in a magical land, where kings and queens lived together in peace and unity, everyday was a festival. A festival of Life, where everyone came together to dance, sing and appreciate the presence of life.

The land gave many fruits and flowers, and therefore the people of the kingdom spend much time outside. On the land side, there was was a simple flower lady who offered her services for the king to maintain collecting flowers for all the festivities. By that she could contribute to the whole kingdom and make enough for a living.

Together with her maids she visits the palast every day to bring the full flower baskets to the ceremonies, where they are first offered to the holy Altar. It is always very early in the morning, there takes a ceremony place that is so beautiful and enchanting that it many thousand people in and lives on to this day.

Sometimes the flower ladies are unnoticed, but the flowers are an essential part of the whole process.

We bring flowers to the priests and they offer them with water and milk to the altar, then we have a festivity of chanting and dancing and thanking for all the gifts that Mother Earth provides us in many folds. The flower lady smiles, with a flowery presence, she loves the attention by the Kingdom who chose her to bring light on the whole ceremony.

Flowers are also very talkative and healing, we can go into the garden and ask a flower what kind of weather will be. Just sit there and breathe, wait and the flower will let you know. So kind and fine, the flowers are subtle and beautiful in nature, just choosing to be fragrant and graceful.

We can also scent a flower and compliment one another with these smells and colours. On likes to go to bed, well then we can choose flowers that are relieving and good for a night, however we are still in the kingdom celebrating so we choose flowers with bright colours and light scents.

The flower lady smiles and starts to dance a little from left to right, Devi is her name and she serves with flowers from her childhood.
You know, everything is changing much, however all the ways we do things are still remaining the same. Even the flowers change a little, yet they remain always one with us, as the ways we do things never change, it is like breathing.

Breathing flowers and dancing in a flower field is my favorite activity, she laughs and grins at us. Come let's go for a walk and I show you my favorite place. It is by a beautiful source, leading into a spring, where the grass is lush and green, the soil holds rich minerals that make the flowers be bright and beautiful - let's go.

So we walk together with Devi through the fields and meadows, around the forests and beside the stream we hear the lush sound of the waters, that lead us to the source. Oh smell, these are my favorite flowers, very special and fine in nature, they are so tender, they hear every word I say. Let's get closer and watch the flowers and ask them kindly for a blessing.

We come closer and see the flowers from a close, with magnificent colours and stunning forms they interact and show the Grace of Creation. We see different ones, red, and purple flowers that are waiting and dancing in the wind. As soon as we see them, we inhale and see, how the flower pedals are slowly opening and showing their inner beauty.

The inner beauty shines with kindness and an unforgettable smell that instantly relieves any disease. We become so attracted, we like to get closer, however there are so many more flowers, it is a whole ocean of flowers, in colours blue and light blue we find flowers that are fine and small, we find gross and solid ones, we find also flowers that have scents that attract butterflies.

There is one in light rose and one in yellow with beautiful punctuation and symbols on the wings, we also see them land inside a flower and disappearing for a moment. It takes a while, but then the butterfly happily flies out and searches for a playmate.

As we sit and watch the butterfly find another butterfly to play, we observe how slowly the rain comes in. A warm and soothing rain covers our head and skin. We feel a rain drop running down our cheeks and along our chin.

The flower lady invites us to dance and play in the rain, as it is like music, we celebrate the serene scene with joy and happiness. Together with the butterflies we dance and sing along to the song of the rain.

It is the rain song, come and sing along, to that beautiful song, come let's sing along.
May all beings be like flowers harmless and kind
With a beautiful smell with the wonderful taste of the divine
Heartily enjoy the colors and the scents,
In nature it is always good to spend
Life is beautiful as is it is - let's pray
So shall it be for every time and day
Let's connect Ourselves to the good way.
Every drop of rain feels so fine and okay.
I might be happy, and in harmony,
With the flowers, the rain, the soil and sun,
I feel like life is blooming and just has begun.

Every breath one takes there Is possibilty to awake
Let's enjoy the travel and give the night a chance,

Prepare with simple breathing and just feel fine and ok.

Like you are laying in a bed of flowers, so soft and tender you sink in, and with every breath there is more space to relax, let's relax into the breath to sink more and more into the bed of flowers. The wonderful feeling holds on and one listens to the breathing, slow and rhythmic in harmony with the body and mind.

Keep the breathing equal and fine and try not to think to much, just enjoy the bed of flowers, Let yourself sink and feel how the body is becoming lighter and lighter, Like a butterfly we become smaller and smaller, we can sense the lightness of the body which transforms into a small, tiny speck of light. We are now this light and it is so light you can be as light as light itself.

Feel the ease and surround yourself with the comfort of the night. Slowly we sense the breathing again and nice fresh air flows into the body, and the light returns back to the bed of flowers.

One is there, just breathing and we invite one of our best friends to come along into the beautiful flower garden with us, there we can roam and play for a while until we are again coming back to our selves.

Just imagine the free space and endless lush field in your imagery flower garden, where a bed of flowers and a friend always wait for you, go and enjoy the space.

When there is the moment to come back, we reconnect with the body and breathe again. The breath is the bridge between the imagery world and the body.

Just breathe and now the breath is always with you, like a good friend, that comes along on a journey to travel with you. Patiently and persistently breathe and feel the ease.

With every breath the lightness within the body spreads from the heart, the center of light, into the whole body. Breathing in and out, equally, will bring balance to the whole body and there we find the space to relax and imagine.

It is like the soil,
The breath,
Like the rain that comes,
The in and out,
It is the flower that grows,
Oh, the Nature knows.
The rhythm equal and steady,
Are you ready?

Say goodbye to the flower lady and follow along to have a nice soothing sleep on your flower bed.

The lady further comes back with a flower garland, beautifully decorated and made of the most fragrant colours of your favorite flowers, coming just to you with a smile, what a present! We smile and keep on the smile into our soothing night, alright.

Let's rest, relax, breathe through and wish for a good, good night.

Security Story

<u>1667 words, 25 minutes</u>

There is a space within the universe where we are all safe and sound. It is the heart of the Absolute Truth, the well-wisher of all beings, as it is the location of the Highest Truth, the one living there is the creator of this universe, with many names and faces, this person gives us shelter in form of a lotus flower.

This Lotus flower is the protection that sits within everyone's heart.

This story my Father always told me, the son Samatura says, smiling and having a glance into the sky, but where is security in the outside world? When I feel insecure, what can I do?

Samatura is now not a little child anymore, he can think and be aware, of certainty and uncertainty. Like us, he knows, there are dangers in the world, but he is brave enough to live a life.

He breathes through and follows the river into the forest where his teacher is situated. Sandapa will know, he is a wise man and contributes to the wellbeing of all his disciples and students, but he is more encouraged to share his message of security and peaceful living in this world.

The question of Samatura still roams in his head, where there is security in me, there also must be security within every one.

Let's prepare to meet Sandapa, who usually sits under a tree in the forest and writes his scriptures and ancient texts. He is living in the forest for his whole life and never had any fight. Living in security and peace he teaches this message for everyone, especially for the Son of the Kingdom who one day will remain in position to lead the kingdom to many more generations.

Sandapa awaits the young disciple and son of the Kingdom with a smile. He is very lean and tall, with bright eyes and tender cheeks, his hear is white and he sits under a tree.

I see, you are walking alone from the kingdom, do you think you are free? Bring a friend to come along with you, therefore security will come true. Sandapa grins and knows all the questions by his disciple. Yet, he invites him to sit for a meditation and we all can join.

Let's find a comfortable position, where we are align with the ground and with the sky. Come to ease in that position and gently close your eyes. Let it be like a window opening for the holy altar.
There, on this altar you see many beautiful deities and pictures of saints, like great masters and mystical beings. See yourself sitting in this holy place and find ease, watching the candle lights and smelling the inscence, so fragrant and nice, the whole room is filled with joy and

happiness. It is secure and safe, therefore we don't have to worry about anything. Just breathe, equally in and out, see the air flowing in regularly, and constant, and see it flowing out, regular and constant.

One is safe, to be breathing means to be in the security of life. Here in the body, we are safe, here in the sacred room we are safe, here with a guide and teacher we are safe. Feel the shelter and open your heart, like a lotus flower. Let this lotus flower bloom and see every petal of this lotus flower adjust to the light.

The light shines from your heart and illuminates the room, the petals of the lotus flower open and one is surrounded by this lotus flower light.

Did you know, that lotus flowers even grow in the deepest swamps, where there is hardly pure water and light? Yet, the lotus flower remains unspoiled and graceful in-midst this nature.

Let's go for a soothing and mild walk down the forest lane to find a swamp with many lotuses. There we see the trees opening up a way for Us, the alley leads straight to a little muddy swamp, where we find a wooden floor. Let's wait here and see the flowers in the distance.

With shimmering silver and purple the petals of the lotuses surround the yellow golden middle, the stigma. It is a splendid wonder to look at, but how can the lotus flower feel safe in this swamp, so dark and moist?

It is a wonderful question, let's explore the answer and ask the Lotus flower, Sandapa smiles and plugs a lotus flower, which he will offer to the sacred altar in the room. He knows the answer already but he promises us to bring this lotus flower into a safe place, where he gives it to the other offerings like fruits and milk to the deities.

While we return, the Lotus flower starts to speak and gives us many interesting answers to our questions.
In a subtle and clear voice the purple-golden Lotus says:
I am secure, when I am within me, as the sun light comes, I open up. I trust, the sunlight is my benefactor bringing me growth.

As the Lotus explains the ways to come to a place of security we share a human place of security we call home, this home is the place where we find community and joy in the things we do, together with our loved-ones, we live here, work, study and find shelter.

Samatura is obliged and puts this beautiful lotus flower on his head, I will bring this back to my father, so I can tell him everything about, what I learnt today with you. Thank you, kindly accept my humble obeisances. Samatura bows in reverence and walks on with a lotus flower on his head.

In a beautiful kingdom, that longed to be at peace,
We can explore and walk around the forest at ease.
There also is a teacher and when we kindly ask, please.

Give us an answer to our questions, bring us release,
The teacher may illuminate the darkness into light.
As long as there is no fight, we are alright.
Let's enjoy this little bit of life, feel and shine bright.
Even, when we have to say goodbye the day and hello to the night.

As always the day ends, in every wonderful kingdom, and eventually there comes the night. In this Kingdom it is tradition to have a safe and sound ceremony, with oil lamps, and a concert. Beautiful and serene at the same time, the students of Sandapa, as well as the Son of the King, Samatura, are joining the good night ceremony with lights and chants.

Samatura chants:

May all beings be at peace,
May all beings find their ease,
Shall all live in harmony,
Peace, Love and Unity.
The trees are watching the stars, the birds are tweeting their songs, together with the stars that illuminate the night, today there shines a special light, it is a full moon show, with special honor to all the Mothers and Teachers.

There, Mother Nature becomes a special thanks and appreciation, there also all the teachers are handed wonderful flower garlands and presents for their service.

All fits together under the beautiful night sky, the mild wind blows into the trees, and makes the leaves start to dance. There is a chance we see Mataja making a sacred fire, one can sit and see the sacred procession of inscence and milk, with flowers and oil lamps, we can also see the holy rivers and streams, that are being honored and everyone from the kingdom joins together in harmony.

We feel safe, and sound on this night.
We can breathe safety and protection. With every inhale there comes safety and with every exhale we let go the uncertainty.
We inhale security, and let go uncertainty with the exhale.
Breathe and feel the security coming to you, and the uncertainty leaving you, more and more we relax and find space to smile.
Let's be happy and celebrate life as it is. Even in this night there certainty, tomorrow the sun will rise, as always, we give thanks to our Mothers and Teachers that help us on our path and we thank Mother Earth for Life.

We now relax our body, with every breath, there comes upon relaxation, of the body, and mind. We are relaxing the head, the head is relaxed, breathe equally in and out, now relax the neck and throat, the neck and throat shall relax, we breathe in and out.

Now let's relax the shoulders and arms, elbows, palms and fingertips, breathing in and out, the shoulders, arms, elbows, palms and finger tips relax.

We shall relax the chest and upper body, inhaling and exhale, we do so. We shall relax the belly and lower back, inhaling and letting go with the exhalation. The whole of the upper body is now relaxed.

Now breathe and relax the thighs, legs, knees, ankles, feet and tippy toes, all the parts of lower body relax with the next inhale and exhale the whole body is relaxed.

Now we calm our thoughts, as we imagine a beautiful light giving us protection and security, this light fulfills our heart and blossoms like a wonderful lotus flower.

This Lotus flower shines in the most wonderful colours and protects us. The light reaches every parts of the body, every cell and we see ourselves in this light, engulfed and surrounded with a healing light of security.

Put your palms together and feel the harmony and security. Feel good and let the breathing be natural. Like a lotus flower, you can now open your hands and bring them to your lotus eyes. Surround your eyes with the healing energy of the hands and let your eyes bathe in the palms of your hands. Breathe, equally in and out. Breathe, just naturally.

Maybe sigh, or massage your head, around the eyes and your jaw to feel totally fine. All is now safe and sound, with a smile we are ready for a good, good night.

Rest, and relax completely.

Tree story

<u>1374 words, 20 minutes</u>

In this mighty Kingdom, once upon a time, there lived the oldest and wisest trees in the world. These trees were so rooted, that no one could shake them, as these trees were holding onto the ground, no one could ever rip them out, no giant, no dragon, no king, nor queen, but they all know, the wonderful humbleness of a tree.

So humble and kind, the tree doesn't care, about all this, the tree is not winning any price, but the honor and respect of all human kind. Even the wind, sometimes tries, but hardly comes to terms with this forest kingdom, where the trees hold onto their roots.

We have to appreciate the tradition and the groundedness of these wonderful ancient beings, that have stood the test of time, further trees evolved with us, and before us, so they know everything about the earths history.

Once in a lifetime of a tree, he has to hold space for birds and humans alike to have a nest. Sometimes, big birds are bringing many sticks and branches to the crown of the tree, to build a nest.

This nest then, is a place for the children, the baby birds and offsprings to gain experience and to grow up. When a bird family is ready, they move into another place, but this can take a long while.

Same with the people of the kingdom who want to live at the feet of the wonderful trees, and therefore sometimes build little huts on the ground to find shelter and security in the woods of this kingdom.

Trees are often so humble, they accept everything that other beings bring to them, even their saws and nails, trees are that tolerant, however one shall treat a tree, like oneself treats a friend.

The friendliness of the trees surely comes back in for of wisdom and inspiration, as the tree breathes out the air, we breathe in and likewise the other way around, we breathe out, the air, that the trees breathes in.

The circle of air, flowing from the lungs of the person, to the plant and other way around is the circle of life. We can feel this, breathing in and breathing out, feeling safety and protection, just knowing the shelter of the trees will be there.

Trees are also very much delighted by our presence, as we come to a tree, we can bow down and greet the tree with happiness and joy. The tree knows, and feels tine with that.

When we humans bring a light or a candle, we have to be very careful, because the tree knows, that this can also hurt us, and of course, it is like the sun light, we are all connected.

So one day, Samatura went into the forest. However, this time he left his kingdom not alone, but he brought a group of friends, that all wanted to meet his teacher, yet the teacher was not sitting as usual under that tree. He must have been for a walk.

So the group around Samatura was curious and wanted to know, what to do in the forest. As we all like to roam and play in the forest, it was unlike that Samatura wanted everyone to sit by the tree and to listen.

Therefore we all sit, with the tree, and however meditating like the tree.

So find a comfortable position and imagine your spine. You see the spine, vertebrae for vertebrae and there is also a root, imagine, the root coming from the lowest bottom of the spine and spreading throughout the soil, into the layers of the ground.
That ground then is the fundament for our balance.

So we breathe, and breathe in the balance. Equally in and out,
Balanced breath, equally in and out.
All in harmony and balance, the breathing flows naturally and the body is align with all the elements. As the spine is straight, we are relaxing our jaw and head. We can let go of any tension, to relax and ease, into a smile.

Breathe and smile, gently.
Breathe and be in balance.
Like the roots of a tree, we find steadiness in the ground.
And we can also tone a sound, that helps us to relax.
Lets open our mouth, wide and full, on AHHH, hold the sound as long as possible. AHHHH
Now breathe again and find the balance and harmony, in the ground, and of course we can tone another sound.
This time for our heart, the Sound goes UHHHH, very mild and long, we can tone this once more, UUHHHH and there you connect to your heart and now lets embrace the smile, lets connect to

our head with HUMMMM, long and gently, sound HUMMMMM. These three sounds, AHHH, UHHH, HUMMM are the essential building blocks of life

Like a tree has a seed, that's the AAH, it also has a stem, that's the UHH, and of course it has a crown and that's the HUMMM.
All together these three sounds AUM give the primal sound, a wonderful invention.

The trees are mostly silent, but they can understand all the sounds of the universe, therefore we always have to be conscious what we say in our environment, as we are peaceful, breathing and meditating, the environment, the trees and all the other beings are very happy with us.

Of course we can smile and find our happiness within our heart. There, a wonderful lotus flower blossoms and we see, that everyone's lotus flower is the same, yet different.

Everyone is breathing the air, yet we are all different from the inside.
All the trees are of the same structure, yet, every tree is one of a kind. Isn't that beautiful?
Let's relax and find out how the trees are embracing the night.

A tree doesn't really need to close the eyes to sleep, yet knows exactly when the sun is setting, therefore around this time, the tree gives everything into the atmosphere, to celebrate and cheer the great gift of life.

Sometimes, a lot of flowers are coming from a tree, sometimes, the tree dances in the wind to find expression, and sometimes the fruits of a tree are growing from just a little seed.

One seed has all the information a tree needs to live on for thousands of years, and even in the nights, the trees are growing upwards and downwards, isn't that interesting?

As all the beings, like the trees are part of this world, we are also growing in the night, yet, we have to be sure, that we are relaxed and ready for the upcoming night. Therefore the trees prepared a nice soothing song for the upcoming good night.

It is again, around that time, where everything sets, from the shine, of the sun, to the son, of a kingdom divine. Please, enjoy the moment, and breathe, like we are here together to live.

Enjoy the moment and breathe,
The air comes in and out,
There is so much doubt,
But leave it all behind,
Be sure and one shall find,
That there is more to the dark,
That there is always a spark,
That ignites the wisdom of life.

Even thought we respect the light,
We know, it must be night,
Whenever we are in sight,
we arrange to be alright,

With a song, that goes all night long.

Sing it and feel it in the breath.
Sing it and feel it in the air,
Breathe and be enjoying the now.
Everything is in care, just trust, just trust.
There is no more, do's or must.
Just relax and keep the breath,
Feel the peace and the ease.
Root yourself to the ground,
And hear the beautiful sound.
It is the air, in the space,
Now imagine a face,
Let it be kind and smile,
Hold it on for a while,
Enjoy the sight,
For a good, good night.

In the moment we listen to the trees, we are also listening to our selves, conscious and wise, we are all rooted on the same earth.
Be kind and bring your friends, to this wonderful kingdom of peace and harmony. Enjoy every bit of it.
Rest and sleep well.

Trust Story

<u>1531 words, 20 minutes</u>

Trust is the true essence of relationship. Sometimes we go blind when so in love, that we trust the world in a child-like feeling as being in the Mothers womb.

Samatura was traveling to the forest with a friend who suddenly asks to stand still and wait. I hear something. It is like a tree is talking to me. Yes, this can happen in the middle of the forest, there might be a tree. Waiting and holding for a breath, Samatura just trusts his friend in curiosity and then suddenly he hears it, too.

There is a voice whispering. Trust me, there is a storm coming, a big thunder rolling in, you better have a shelter, somewhere in the kingdom, trust me, a storm is coming.

Samatura and his friend are looking at each other and agree, to trust the tree.

Hey, we are free, but being pulled away by a storm, we can see, is better to come inside and wait it out.

Very protected and safe the home of the palast is waiting for them. Both of the young boys are walking down the wild forest lanes, looking into the distant lands. Somehow, Samatura feels now, what the tree was saying, the weather is changing, even though they still see people walking and playing on the streets.

Trust the tree and worry for your friend and yourself, as everyone worries for the close one and oneself, everyone is in care. Let's find the way back to the kingdom's garden.

There are always some signs that a storm or weather is coming up, and there we can learn something here. There are flowers, called the weather flowers, that instinctively close their petals as soon as something comes up. Same with weather trees, weather frogs

and weather people, that intuitively know what is going to happen.
Just trust, and you will be alright,
Even when there is no storm in sight,
Please trust the beings around you,
As one says it honestly it sounds true.
Truth and trust ring a bell,
Let's all trust and be well.
There is intuition in every cell,
One might be the one to tell.

So trust yourself and find a way,
Speak it out, and be the One to say,
Let's change, let's awake and hey,
There might be another beautiful day.

So Samatura and his friend trusted the tree and thank god they arrive early in the kings Palais where everyone wondered where have you been. Oh what a surprise and the first drops come down, thanks to the tree, we made it early. Thanks to the tree?

Yes, we heard the tree speak, so subtle and fine he whispers, there might be a storm, better come home, better go now. There might be a storm, trust. And we trusted ourselves and the tree, so kind and humble bowed to thee.

Now, we are happy, waiting for the storm in security. Possibly, there is a chance that we might be watching this storm for days on end, but that's life in protection and with a friend.

Samaturas Friend smiles and gives a cheerful song from his lips.

There once was a kingdom, no storm could shake, just the right time to awake and we find ourselves in the midst of the mystical forest, where trees can talk and animals can walk.

Every day here is a festival, we celebrate the sensations of Mother Nature, the endless changes, that come and go.

Let's sit with your teacher and meditate.

Also in the Kings palast there are many rooms for once in a while the teacher comes by to read and study the scriptures with the young boys from the kingdom, already so brave and wise, they know nature, but they also shall know the divine.

There is Life in every being, the teacher says, there is life in every cell. Therefore we can sense all the body with just a thought.
Now, instantly, I can know how my little toe is doing, just by thinking of this part of the body.
There is intelligence in the whole body. Let's try.

Bring yourself to ease and breathe. Do you feel your tippy toes? Breathe and relax, there is awareness, so energy in the little toe, the first toe, the second toe, the third toe and the fourth toe. Do you see and feel? Be aware, that energy is now filling the space in your feet and breathing makes it happen.

Breathe and feel again, your toes are alive and relaxed. Now feel your whole feet- Be aware of the energy at the feet. Be aware of the ankle and of the whole leg. Now of the thigh, the root of the spine and the whole spine. Breathe and feel into the body, now your whole lower body is relaxed and filled with awareness. Sense the trust and the security, be aware of the belly and now imagine you find shelter in a deep, deep cave made of rose crystals.

Imagine walking into this crystal cave of light and glowing crystal quartz in rose. One can see the reflection and the beautiful splendor of the rose, it is a whole cave with nice rose colored walls, all surrounding you. One finds a place in the crystal cave to sense the stability and protection. Just trust and feel safe.

The whole of your body is in union with the awareness and we start to be breathing slower and slower, we are becoming finer and finer and with every breath we are becoming lighter and lighter. Our whole upper body is now filled with peaceful and radiant light. From the belly it radiates to all the parts of the body. The chest is filled with awareness and we feel the chest. There is a room, where we meet our friend, and kindly greet our friend with a smile. Smile and feel the friendship eternally from the heart. The whole heart and the upper body are now illuminated with the light of friendship.

Just breathe and feel the sensations coming and going, sense the air and know every storm also might pass. The air comes and goes again. All is coming and going, but we are here, right now in safety and peace. Now relax your head with the light of peace. Peace be with every part of the head and jaw. All is illuminated in peaceful light of relaxation.

The whole head relaxes and we find absolute serenity in the breath. Breathing equally in and out, all is in care, all is fine and we find the ease.

The Storm is outside and is now noticeable as the two boys thank each other and the teacher for the serenity.

Let's together speak a prayer for the kingdom and for the whole world.

May all beings in this kingdom and the whole world be happy and at peace.
May all beings be at peace and happy.
May we all find absolute serenity.
May there be trust and happiness all around,
May we find the inner voice that guides us,
Torwards peace, love and unity.

Trust starts with trusting one self. This trust to oneself comes from the knowledge who we are and what really is. With meditation, says the teacher, we can learn how life really is.
It is like the storm sometimes, unknown, behind the clouds, and as it is coming, sometimes in the air, and then eventually passing away again.

Thank you, dear teacher, Samatura and his friend Dandilion are happy that they are inside now, whereas the storm is breaking down and it might take awhile for the storm to ease and rest again, but it is almost night and the thoughts are easing with a glass of warm cow milk and they talk about the good adventures that they experienced in the forest.

Do you remember taking this bow and sticks into the forest and you shot this apple off my head, precisely, like always? It was just a practice shot from very close, next time we do it, I have to be 3 kilometers away, not 2. Yes, maybe the tree can help us prepare, as I know they are very calm and steady.

I love these trees, says Samatura with a smile, they give me so much space to play, I might never grow up around a forest tree like that. That's the way, agrees his friend. Trust your inner Child, it might be the most precious livelihood one has.

Let's enjoy the milk and head to bed. Yes, we are all calming down and dreams may come true. All is in care and the boys from the kingdom are willing to maybe one day find a unicorn, as there are many mysteries in this forest, there also is a story of a unicorn, but that might rest for another time. Now, we prepare for sleep with a trusting light, that fully surrounds our body for good sleep. From head to toe, and from toe to head. Feel and relax. Now the whole body is relaxed. Ease in and find your sleep. Sleep well.

Water Fountain story

<u>1518 Words, 25 minutes</u>

Once upon a time there was a market place with a wonderful water fountain in the midst of it. The water fountain was known to heal and protect the masses from diseases and cure old age and fogetfulness. This water fountain never stopped to talk, as it springs and springs, water comes from its mouth, deep from the earth. In the well there are many coins for good fortune and the well is always visited even into the night.

The market place did not know any rest, it was just as busy as always and good business one was making here for sure, as there are so many people attracted to this spring the water flows and so business flows. One day, there came the king into town with all his consulates and He was busy with business, but he had to visit the sacred water fountain for once to see, if there is healing possible for a friend.

The king bowed before the water source and asks kindly, please can you give us release from this sickness, my friend he is very weak and surely doesn't want to die, but he wants to live.
With a tender gesture the king unfolds his hands and the water fountain embraces him with a dear sound.

Please take a cup and bring it to the friend, he shall drink from me. Half with his eyes closed and then bring him to my friend, the warm spring in the mountains. There he can find relieve and be at peace and serenity. He shall find his relieve within a short period of time.

Even the king did not know about this termal source in the mountains, but he surely wants to find out and bring his friend to out. Hot springs are natural appearances of bringing hot water from the earth into a bath.
The king went back to his friend and wonders already happened. He was suddenly relieved. The king was so in

fascination that he asks how can this be, we did not even go to the spring in the mountains. How can this be?
Spring in the mountains? Yes, there is a hot thermal spring in the mountains near by. Let's go and see.

The two friends now intrigued by the wonder of the source, really want to find out, what is behind the mysterious water source. Life is like a springing Source of happiness and livelihood, of many possibilities, so abundant and free.

So the two, the king and his friend, on the way to the thermal springs and there they met two pilgrims. I wonder where you are going, you must be the king, what a surprise! There are many ancient temples in these mountains and in the land there are many mysterious creatures, like speaking trees, or unicorns, so what are you looking for exactly?

The king, in a friendly says: We are following the Water and only the water,

because it is the most holy of all the elements.
Just imagine, our whole body is water and in tune with the elements. Know that everything in life is connected to the water into the light. So let's Pilger together to that water source.
On the way the four pilgrims and counter an old lady. She seems to be looking for herbs or any other kind of flowers in the forest. Maybe she knows where the fountain is.

Oh yes, the fountain is very close, one can almost hear it from here. Listen in and one can hear the fountain from a far. Be calm and listen. The soothing sound of a fountain appears and also one can notice a river that is just near by.

The soothing sound of water, the endless river streams.
All comes from a source that we keep in our dreams.
The mystical forest, the fountain of life, they all spring

With happiness and joy into life one can sing.

With the help of the water, everyone can be healed, with the help of the water, one can refresh and rejuvenate,. As we let it flow in the search to grow, there might be the sound we hear, there might be the crown of no fear, so we know, we are on water. We are all water.

Let's embrace the sounds and no fear of the grounds we are safe where we are the soothing elements always in balance always in harmony. The king and his friend and the pilgrims were now so close to the water source that they could not even understand their own words yet's it was clear that the thermal bath is just here. The king-size of leave finally we have found the mysterious source of the hot Springs. The spring seem to be healing I can feel it already. Now let's find a way to get into the bath. The pilgrims please stop for a devotional chant

Oh healing water, the source of life.
It also is warm what a surprise come, long and enjoy the endless stream can you hear the flow and the singing of the birds who are so happy that we are here now let's relax and have no fear. Now relax the whole body and imagine you are sitting in this wonderful hot spring constantly going into the bath we are sitting in and leaving into the nature becoming a river stream. There he sits and we find ourselves to be at ease. All healing want to please please please, take all our dirt.

So cleansing and pure. We breathe in and out again. Equally in an equally out again. The king is happy and now says this spring of hot water shall be protected for the ever lasting stream of people coming here for healing and rejuvenation. Let's make this a natural paradise for everyone to see and you pilgrims you shall be the guards of this place as you love the water more than anyone. The pilgrims so delighted and happy know their duty is set.

As all the participants of the party listen to what the source says, suddenly it starts to speak: watch I am not the only one. There are more like me coming out of the ground making this precious sound up in the very hills deep in the caves there are more springing sources hidden. Like the fountain of the marketplace and the hot fountain here in the mountain there are many more of these precious springs. Some of them are yet to be explored and who has time and the courage to go can find them.

Now let's sit and meditate here at the source and feel how the water is cleansing you from within and from without.

Breathe and feel the pure rejuvenation that comes from the source, slowly and gently the water treats us well.

Be aware of the sound of the water and an endless rhythm sounding the vibration of life and making us happy just like that - it is joy, it is harmony, it is peace. Relax and find the ease within this piece. The water is also a body for the most part so we give thanks to the water.

We can also harmonize our system which is mostly water.
So within and without the water can help us for a good rest. As we appreciate the water we can harmonize and bring everything into balance. Water is balance. Let's embrace this harmony and balance of the water, wherever it may be. To be sure we can say water is with us but it doesn't belong to anyone it is free, always flowing. Always in the flow like the breath. So these elements, Water and air are like friends that like to explore and be together.

Together the air and the water are in union.
Now relax your whole body and the water in the soil and all the elements it is now time to rest and to bring full relaxation from the hand to the head to the chest to the belly to the feet. All of

the parts of the body are now relaxed and in harmony like the water like the air that is constantly coming into the nostrils and going out of the nostrils.
Just equally breathe and let yourself return to the kingdom within.

The kingdom of your body is now safe and relaxed, fully conscious of all you are doing. Every sensation is equally part of your being and you find comfort and the little space of your heart. Where an endless fountain of good dreams is springing into the night.
As all are returning, we gently close our eyes and find the ease of the breeze. In and out, equally, coming and going. Just gentle and soft, the night shall be the river in which the fountain of joy and happiness springs.

Let's pray for all the beings, for all the water and for the every single drop of happiness in this universe.

May All be happy and well, may we all have a good night and sleep alright.

Creativity Story

<u>1483 words, 20 minutes</u>

To be creative means to truthfully use the energies that make creation. Now let's create a beautiful garden where we just sit in and meditate for the rest of our whole life. For the rest of our lives and for the life beyond we can create a life and life beyond. Everyone is the creator of their lives possibility, balance and harmony and eventually of their unity.

This might be a creative garden of unity so let's take our creative tools which are our imagination, it is like dreaming, and let's imagine ourselves on the wonderful green fields. One is sitting there with their eyes half open and half closed. We are there just breathing and doing nothing else. No worries about nothing, everything is in care, we are breathing we are alive, everything is there. Even though our friends are here with us and they can help with creating a beautiful

garden of unity - let's imagine togetherness.
There may be a fountain in the middle of the garden which springs and brings creative water, so pure and fine, we are able to witness the water fountain also to create a ripple, into a stream, a small, beautiful river stream and we sit in this garden just breathing.

We witness and we become the playful creator of our garden of unity.
So what can bring us more into balance and peace? May it be our friends and family, let's bring them all here and see they are happy as we are happy, too. So we are sitting in this garden of unity and we are breathing and we are happy.

 Let there also be nice flowers because everyone likes to smell nice flowers, and you can imagine many flowers in many colours, in red and in orange, and yellow, in blue and in rose and in purple. There is also a nice and wonderful rainbow hovering from one side with the sun over to the other side with the fountain creating a nice and lush rainbow in this garden of unity.

So there might be a happy family and friends and some nice animals. Whichever animals you like. This is the power of creativity, to imagine, everything is a possibility and everything is possible. Now you can be creative on your own. Just do as you like and form, shape, create the world as you like it to be. And you can see creativity which is with you and for all.

Just give yourself the space and allow yourself to be creative. Then creativity can blossom like a flower and it can spring like a fountain into the world. In any colour, in any shape. Of course we want to use it for something good, that's why say unity, because it is always good, bringing people together, joining friends and family and all being in happiness and peace.

Let's all be happy and creative. In our mind and our hearts we can be creative with our hands and likewise be healthy. We can be healthy and creative with our whole body. We can be joyful then in a place of harmony with our full being. We can be the creator of the garden. Caring, Creating, how to know, is all in your head and in your dreams. Let's meditate and see the creative flow of life that is coming from the hearts and going again. But as coming from the belly creativity is surrounding the whole being. This is everywhere and everything.

It is the light, it is the water, it is the fire and it is the earth and the air. Creativity is everything. It is music, it is our way to express the voice. So we can express the voice and listen to our own music. For us to be content and with it to be creative, means to be content. The voice the music and what we do is creativity, so all you see and all you feel, or all you touch. This is one Creation, and where does this creation come from?

It is all within the self, within the body, mind and spirit, so lets explore the mysterious world of creativity.

We sit silent and equanimous in the Garden of Unity and feel at home, just like that. Breathing, equally in and equally out. Our place in this Garden is always there and we can always come back here as we wish. Just bring your awareness to the heart and here you are in the garden of unity. Now let's breathe and find a huge brush, a magic brush that allows us to brush with our eyes and paint in all the colours we like. We can brush with our eyes and paint it all. We may paint from the top of the head, to the right, to the bottom and to the left, we paint all around in circles and we can twinkle with our magic creative eye brush. Twinkle and paint, how you feel like.

The feelings are like to motor of our creativity. It is driving our creativity and bringing life to our creation. So when we feel grounded and close to earth, our creation might appear in a brown or red. When we are happy and joyful, it might appear in an orange or light gold, as we are all creators one can co-create with a friend. It is easier to make rainbows as together one has more creative freedom.

The source of creativity comes from our belly, from the connection to our Mothers and the connection to our Mother Earth. One can nurture this connection by breathing into the belly, slowly and gently in and softly letting go. Put one hand on the belly and feel how the air is steaming into the body and belly lifting up, like a balloon. The belly is lifting up and the air circulates in the belly. Just focus on the breathing and the ups and downs of the belly. It is coming like waves, rising and passing, rising up inhale and passing away, exhale. Let this be rhythmic and equal. Equally in and out again. Gently in and out again. The breathing is balanced and equal, our mind is steady and peaceful. We celebrate every breath and feel the ups and downs. From the source, the connection to one's Mother energy can flourish and we imagine a beautiful bright orange flower blossoming. So bright and beautiful it blossoms into every direction, to the left and right, the below and high, the belly feels fine and the orange blossom opens every single petal for a wonderful light.

One can see this light flowering and opening further and further the light expands and a golden shimmering glow enlightens the whole body. All the body parts are now surrounded in golden light of creativity, with a smile we can acknowledge and find serenity.

We breathe and by breathing the golden smile and the light expands even further into the atmosphere where it spreads and comes to life. Creativity in person is now alive and we have the chance to greet and welcome the creativity we see, a person wearing a gold cloak, surrounded with beautiful shimmering light. This person is just here for us, bringing us peace and joy.

We shall walk in the garden of unity to find a nice place for the sunset, where the rainbow meets the horizon there is also the sun setting for a good night. Therefore we trust the creative world, our creative world and we follow along to seek out a nice and comfortable place for the sunset celebrations. The birds are tweeting, the bees are humming and all is in care, the creation is now in full swing, changing, like the seasons, like we change our garments, from golden to blue, to purple and into the night.

There might, there might be the light of the setting sun, creative as always, it creates a scene of splendor and serenity, the celebration of light to transform into the night.
That's right, let's celebrate this way with a smile and appreciation. Thank you dear sunshine, thank you Mother Earth, that I am here and alive. Thanks for everything, for all the friends, for the family, and for the garden of unity.

Thanks for the birds that sing and everything like the stars and the moon, like the heaven and the air we breathe. Breathe in and relax for a good night. The foremost last sun beams set the sky into colours and like a huge hand has created a wonderful picture, creation is always in flow, ever changing with the eternal glow. One might never forget to thank.

All my thanks to the world,
All the love into the world,
All the happiness and kindness,
All the Unity.

May All beings experience unity and happiness.
May all be free to do, to be, creative and alive.

Let it be a good, good night.
Rest and sleep well.

River Story

<u>1507 words, 20 minutes</u>

Once upon a time there was a river of milk. It was a precious river flowing through the land with the bees and the flowers living in harmony with the human kind. The land was so rich and abundant all the beings were happy and at peace. The river of milk was coming from the source up in the highest mountains. The source was well hidden and no one could reach the source, only by guidance of the priest. This guidance can only be attained when one is humbly serving the whole of the community. So once in a lifetime when a member of the community was giving birth the priest went up to the mountains to fetch a silver cup of milk from this source. This milk was considered holy in this land and it became the link to the divine. This connector called nectar was purified and so rich in minerals it could bring the newborn child to live more than 100 years. In this life time one just has to do the service and one also has to obey the principles of the community like no harming, so being peaceful, and no stealing, in general being of good attitude and peaceful character. One could also be initiated into the livelihood as a monk who'd so be able to drink from the source of all life.

One day it came rain from the heavens and all the people were wondering why is it white rain? It was a special day only every 500 years there is an occasion in the sky where the Milky Way beats with me the rhythm of the milky River like two heartbeats in synchronicity.

So now in this land there was a river of milk flowing and the rainfall bringing new life to the land where the river could not reach and everyone was celebrating the present of life, growing fruits and crops and all one needs for life so one could sustain and live happy and peaceful. When one grows older one can bathe in the river. It is possible that one can be in the river, we just have to imagine it and believe.

With the breathing we can bathe, we can breathe in the stream of peace and purity. This pure and peaceful stream can flow in and around us and protect us and also make us young to live a long life. The ancient Scriptures say that the pool holds the nectar of immortality. This nectar was once brewed on the occassion of creation, where the guides of the heavens came together to brew a milky soup of endless life. A great recipe needs great cooks.

So the best cooks in the whole universe came together to create the world with the help of one special ingredient. It is in the Milky Way and it is always growing from the river. It is a brilliant, most fragrant ingredient that one can find nearby, very close actually, in colours that are pure and translucent, sometimes it has a protection though and one has to be careful to obtain this precious ingredient.

So the Gods were collecting it and bringing it to the soup of Milk where all the heaven guides were watching the process happening and of course the steam was rising from the heat that was made by the eternal flame provided from the ever-lasting woods, from the mystical forests.

Brewing this sacred soup of milk it yet had to be churned, so there came the Mother of All beings with a golden spoon to churn the wonderful mixture into existence and therefore all the creation came into play. This is why the sun and earth are rotating, anyway, this is why this land has a river of milk, because in this process there had to be someone trying this mixture and the youngest one was first.

So one got a silver cup and filled it in. This filling was the first source of the Milky stream that momentarily still flows in the sacred land of immortality. This river of milk is also with us, we just have to breathe and one can feel that this river comes into existence with every breath. The wonderful story dates back to the reign of the first Gods and Godesses that create the Milky Way, in a long way, they made the animals, plants and all beings harmonize by giving all the beings some sort of nectar.

This nectar is still in flow, and through long and persistent service for the community attainable. One can taste this nectar and also dive into the vast milk ocean, where the river of milk ends in. This is a long way of constantly doing good for others an obeying the rules and regulations of the saintly ones, like Father and Mother.

Mother Earth is still churning this Giant Milk Soup and we are all a part of this process, breathing and living gives the texture and serving gives the taste. It is essential like breathing and one can be in happiness, like the people of the lands with the milk river flows.

From that land there is a warrior who earned his livelihood by achieving super feats like holding the breath for long times to dive with the underwater creatures or he got to very high mountains just to meet the angels living there. He renounced fighting long-time ago to celebrate life and learn how to be immortal, hence he came to the land of the Milky River. Wherever he walked people were curious, what does such a fierce warrior do here? He is not fighting but he is looking for something.

A small boy came up to him asking what is going on and why the search, and the warrior in full surrender bows to the young one to tell him, that he hears the sound of the river every night in his dreams and he just closed his eyes to follow the stream of sound, therefore he came here to the land of immortal milky river streams. The boy smiles and suggest him to go to the local priest, he is the father of the village governor and the chief of the river protection program. There is a milky river protection program house just down the road, find the Priest Avalan there.

Avalan is of great statue and a wise man with a calm gaze, please have a seat and lets prepare my favorite tea. The warrior did not come for tea, but he knew waiting in patience is good service. So he waits and the tea is ready, it is a welcome tea Avalon says, as one travels so far just to come here, we are heartily welcoming our guest with a warm tea and later you can have a warm milk. Everything here is making us live a long and healthy life, you know, the fresh air and the purity of the river, all give us a good day and night. This happens every day, and night, hence we seem to be living immortal.

There is a story of trader who wanted to sell all his gold for a glass of this milk and he came here with his whole family. When he arrived he was surprised, he did not even have to trade anything, he just received a nice glass of rejuvenating milk. Then he started to laugh and dance and sing. What a scene, he was so happy, immortal in that sense of joyful and at total ease. Happy and at peace.

Another time there came a beggar here and he was just thirsty, what a surprise it must be hard walking up these hills, isn't it?
The warrior nods and finds his cup already full again, please drink and have some more. There is plenty, it is an abundant source up there, but we are keeping it for the newborn who drink a cup of this milk and remain always young at heart. Young at heart, smiling, and kind. Compassionate with all beings and ever living in harmony.

Just breathe and relax, also for the night you can stay by the river and in the morning you might take a dip in this holy place. Totally happy the warrior sips and listens to the wise man talk, yet Avalan knows it's almost sunset and the night comes in, he better prepares and brings his children to bed, there is also a little celebration with candle lights and butter lamps. These are especially beautiful at night. Watch the ceremony with me please, and join for a warm milky treat, into the Milky Way.

Now two strangers became friends and the warrior forever lived on in this land of immortality to help the priest lighting the candles and butter lamps. In a lifetime of good service and with Love and devotion one can be free, to live in peace, love and harmony.

Enjoy the endless stream of happiness and rest, sleep well and dream on.

Friendship Story

<u>1491 words, 20 minutes</u>

Friends are the essence of life. Let's embrace that and find ourselves in healthy and nurturing relationships as friends and maybe even as long life friends.

Relax your body and find yourself safe and secure in the space of love. Around you, you're being surrounded with a shimmer of light that glows and brings about peace and harmony. This light we breathe and we can feel.

The light of friendship is like the smile. You can see it as soon as you smile honestly, one smiles back. This light of your love, smiling, is the power of friendship. Let's embrace that and find ourselves calm, breathing, feeling and breathing's fully out again. The breathing is equal and the in-breath matches the out-breath. The breathing is natural and the constant flow is audible. You can hear the breathing coming in and going out.

Now you can close your eyes and find yourself in this space of imagination where you sit comfortable on green moss so mild like a cushion and so soft that you sink into this place and it may be a place of peace and harmony. So as you are. Breathing in and equally breathing out again. There's nothing to worry about, we are just trusting the love of nature and the friendship of our breath as our breath is our long life friend.

Smile and say hello to the breath. Embrace the breath. And let the breath go again. It's a constant coming and going. And whatever is happening around you, find yourself always be in balance with the breath as the rhythm goes.

The rhythm might be fast and one can notice if the life is fast right now in this moment, or the breath might be slow, maybe life might be of a slow moment right now. So whatever moment is happening is happening in the breath. The breath is our friend and one might know when to say hello as the friend is coming again and again. And one also knows to welcome the breath with joy and with a smile.

Oh hello you wonderful breath of life, you are my friend coming home. Then there is space for celebration, for love and for life. This is the life happening within you. When the life has happened we have to say goodbye again. This goodbye is a chance to make room and to let go, maybe this friend likes to go with the present.

Like here, bring the peace and take this love, and maybe here you have a smile for your way out. So we let go and the ever-lasting friends go away with love and peace and a smile. When your friend has left, there is enough space to embrace for another time your friend will come.

Breathe in and let your friend the life air come into the nostrils and let your friends go again leaving the nostrils. Every time we breathe we have the chance to equip our friend with a message, and whatever this message may be, one can come up with the one, message going into the world.

This is why we can speak in prayer for the world. This is why we can hope for friendship in the world. Hence we speak it out, and devotion and love. Let's pray.

May all beings be happy,
may all beings be at peace,
may all beings be friends,
like the best friends one can be.

To enhance the potency of this prayer we can speak it louder and we can speak it more often, so one can repeat that prayer again and again.
May all beings be happy
May all beings be at peace
May all beings be friends.

So we are still sitting on the most in a beautiful friendship garden and in this garden there is much friendliness, even the birds, the bees and the trees. And so we could just sit here when all of the beings come to us, and we can greet them with a smile.

The beings smile back in this world's unity, in this garden the friendship is present. Let's also think about our real life friends, let's imagine them and invite them kindly with a smile. All we see, them smiling back and there we go, let's be together in this Garden of friendship.

The sun is shining and the weather is nice, we are able to enjoy the sound of the birds and the song of nature. It is like a concert just for us, the music is so beautiful and harmonious we find our balance here.

See now and it's a blessing, we are here. Now, let's embrace that and feel the breath again. Notice the breath streaming in the nostrils and out again, and find the rhythm to be equal, and the heartbeat in synchronicity.

This synchronicity feels so good to us, it is like a shelter, coming home, to the garden of friendship. We can walk around now and search for something that is interesting for us. Maybe we find the tree with special leaves, or maybe we find a flower with this specific cense, but we do really, is just observing.

We see ourselves playing, we see ourselves wondering in the forest full of adventure, we are witnessing the constant stream of life, like rivers and water flow and our friends they like to be with us.

So together we are exploring this friendship garden, so together we are exploring our friendship, so together we are living in harmony. There is no fight, there's just the pulse of life, that makes us live and feel encouraged, and it makes us smile and happy to be who we want to be.

Let's embrace that and let's embrace the breath, let's embrace our friends and the place we are playing in. This place is in our heart so let's embrace the heart. From this place, it also is in our minds so let's embrace the mind and the imagination. Let's embrace our friends and family and let's embrace the whole world as friends and family.

Now see yourself in this friendship garden and from your heart there is a silver light shining into the hands and the hands embrace each other, bringing the palms together, and now the light shines from the middle of your head into the wide wide world.

May all beings be friends, playing in the friendship garden. May all beings be happy, may all be at peace.

So let's find the breath again and the breathing goes in and out, with saying hello to the breath and with a goodbye we are letting the breathing go.

Everything is in harmony and now in this friendship garden we have time to celebrate, so let's bring everyone together and celebrate this friendship.

The birds are bringing their favorite songs, the elephants are bringing their favorite foods, the monkeys are bringing their favorite bananas, the ducks are bringing their favorite dress. The trees that bring their favorite flowers and the flowers bring their favorite cense. The bees are bringing their favorite honey and all the friends are coming together.

There is a wonderful celebration for the sunset, waiting for the night as the sun brought his favorite friends the moon. And the moon brought her favorite friends the stars, and the stars brought their favorite friends the Stardust. In this Stardust is a wonderful dream to the nice night as it is coming just while the sun sets.

All the animals, all the people, all the flowers and the insects as well as the

sun and the moon are now watching and we are here to all speak a prayer together:
May all beings be happy
May all beings be free
May all live in harmony in this friendship garden.

We are gently closing the night as everyone gently says goodbye with a smile, we also smile and put our palms together again to give thanks. We close our eyes and be content with this wonderful friendship garden where we can return every time even in the night.

Now relax your whole body and feel the life of your breath slowly and gently calming and becoming smooth. Now find yourself in peace and harmony with all the beings around.
 May it be a good night. May the stars shine bright, it's the moon singing a song for peace and harmony. Rest relax and sleep well.

Everything in life is free,

the friendship, the breathing,
the peace and harmony.
We come to this life
With the help of the light.
From the stars and sun,
Life can sprout and begun.

Everything in life is free,
The stars and the sun,
The peace and harmony,
To hold it dear kind,
Is just a state of mind,
To bring it forth and go,
We are the one to know.

Everything in life is free,
The peace, love and harmony.

Mermaid story

<u>1508 words, 20 minutes</u>

Once upon a time there was a Harbor city and three young salesmen that were doing their sales on the sea. Sailing from one continent to another to collect the most precious stories. Together they were sitting at the harbour and wondering where the journey will be going.

One of them was Chris, and Chris loves the orient so he wanted to go to the desert lands, anywhere close to the pyramids and the forgotten Harbour cities of the ancient empires. The other one, Momo, he wanted to go to the faraway lands of India and the Pacific ocean, where there are many stories to be told. The third one, J, wanted to go to the south, where there are many paradise islands with nice people and endless coconuts.

With this journey and to decide where to go, they needed help, so they asked the mermaid for help. She was living in an underwater cave just close to the harbour. And every time she sang a beautiful song, where she was praising the wonderful world's of this Neptune's Union.

This place is hidden under the water and is just reachable by the guidance of the water friends. So one of the three adventurous explorers right away starting begging the mermaid asking how can we reach this place. Neptune's union holds many mysteries and stories and the three were very engaged in finding this place.

The mermaid said: Make sure you have the right attitudes of collecting stories and only collecting stories. Then I will make the preparations for your adventure. So the three promise, clearly understanding the preparations for the adventure and only stories might be collected.

With this preparation the three also had to prepare for the underwater, so they were crafting an undersea bubble. It is the bubble of light with an infinite breath. It is the bubble around the head and it can support long long times underwater. It is an imaginary bubble of breath, but it works just like the normal one.

So there are three adventurous young friends collecting stories for now and later, on their way to explore the mermaid's advice, to go to Neptune's union. With the help of the mermaid the three are diving deep into the blue blue ocean and deeper and deeper until the mermaid says, here that's the entrance.

The entrance is beautifully decorated and two mermen with a bright gaze looked at the three adventurous seafarer. The mermaid explains, these three are here to hear the best stories of Neptune's union so please let them in. They will remain only in peace and serenity as these three will do no harm.

Please show them the wonderful world of this mighty place. The mermen are astonished and open the entrance for the three adventures. The mermaid says now you are on your own.

The first story they hear is via a simple underwater worker. He is busy collecting shells for the underwater celebrations as these shells serve as instruments, as musical instruments. Even the high priests blow these shells for big ceremonies, and the worker tells them how he has to be careful to select only the prettiest and best shells. But eventually when the work is finished he goes back to his family to find everyone safe at home.
 When everyone is welcome, they go for the market. The three companions are very happy to hear the story, because they love markets. Now they're heading onto the market to hear more stories. You are well invited to join for the market since the working is over I can get you there.

At the markets the mermaids and mermen are in full swing bringing goods like underwater spices, plankton, shells and all other gifts from the underwater world to the people. The sharing is caring, he says and we talk to a local underwater salesman who was very delighted to see salesmen from the overwater world.

The world's maybe different but the trading is the same, it is like a constant coming and going like the waves of the shore of the ocean. With a breeze maybe the tides they come and go. Like the breathing coming and going.

We are happy to hear and now proceed to the middle of the market where there is this stage and we listen to an underwater artist chanting a beautiful underwater song.
Under the sea, all be happy, all be free, to eternity, happy and free, and we and the winds, and the union of all the water around Neptune.

Next we are visiting a school of the Neptune Union, in midst the underwater caves, says the mermaid merchant: He bows and tells a story of how he established a school here in the underwater world. I saw many schools in my times on the shores of the earth and I knew education and a safe learning environment is important, so I funded this school with the help of the Union.

It is a blessing that even Neptune himself came to the school to see the children play and learn. This is the way, let's walk it together and one can see a beautiful building carved into the underwater caves and there, very well protected, play the children around in an underwater schoolyard.

The school is visited by sea turtles, little children fish, tiny sharks and whales as well as mermaids and mermen that serve here as teachers. Education and sea knowledge is important, because did you know that more than 70 percent of this body and equally of the earth is a body of water?

Water is the element of balance and serenity. With the help of the land it is holding the balance of all beings. Some sciences believe that the first creature ever living on earth came from the ocean. The vast ocean and the sea are salty, where as the lakes and springs are sweet. What would you say is the taste of water?
Maybe have a cup of water, because water is necessary in our everyday life.

Everyone shall love and appreciate the water, as we do. Here we learn to embrace the water and to keep It clean. We are also collecting findings in the sea, like wracks or treasures. Other things we are upcycling again, so it can be used for ones benefit. Some of the school materials are recycled, we can do a lot and help to keep the planet beautiful.

We also like beautiful things that's why we play music, make art or dance. Everyday there is a sunset festival, where we celebrate the world of the water and the light.

This is a spectacle and you are free to join us into the night. Merman and mermaids like to party and then head home to have good night stories read by the wise fathers and mothers. These are the best way to have a soothing and calm night.

Sometimes Neptune comes by to witness the festivals and there are many stories around his personality. One knows he is of fair blue skin with a big crown on his head, he likes to enjoy the arts and music, even one time he left his throne to dance with the little ones and gave his favorite speech after.

We all have to be wise and conscious of the breath, he said, we have to be wise and conscious of the behavior and therefore let's embrace that, first with the breath. It is the air that connects us all, living beings and it is the water and the light, lets come to unity with all the beings under and over waters, let's make the first step and invite people into our Union.

This is why we are, also, to craft a relationship of friendship from under the sea to the earth and sky alike. All beings shall live in harmony and peace. Let's play and sing together into the sunset. The night is coming.

We are all beings here on earth, living for service and kindness, bringing the world together, thank you, that you are here. It is a blessing and a wish, to bring all the world to unity.

The dance and songs are going into the night and we are breathing through, as the three explorers are on their way upwards to the surface, what they have heard is worth more than just one story, and everyone had their favorite part of the under water world, what was yours?

Let's get back to land and give thanks to the mermaid that gave us entry into this wide world of discovery and let's thank Neptune's Union to bring a new perspective into the night, maybe we dream on and there we prepare and relax the whole body.

From the head to the tippy toes, we relax the whole being and find ourselves in serenity and peace. All is in Union, as we come to Balance and Harmony:

A good night this one shall be. Rest, relax and sleep well.

Sea Travel Story

<u>1487 words, 20 minutes</u>

In times of Travel one can discover the Self.

Once upon a time there were three friends, Chris, Momo and Jo, who all loved the sea as they lived most of their lives in a Harbour city. Trading was their great gift and finding good stories their duty. They all wanted to go around the world but only now it is possible, as they have left home to set sail for an adventure around the world. First the three friends had come over the home sickness, therefore they collected their favorite stories of their families and friends to carry them always home while on the sea.

The sea is full of fish but there also other beings like mermaids and underwater cities. There are also hidden treasures and interesting findings like new species. One has to be careful, and very attentive with the sea and the waters, as the waters are precious and sensible. After all the sailing the three friends believe to protect the sea as much of a part as travel by sea with the wind and with the weather, we are all depending.

Dependent of the water because essentially we are water. The three step on board over the plank onto a wooden sailboat with five masts. The boat is named Hernanda, and has sailed the seven seas many times. The seven seas are also now in sight for the three adventurers. As long as we are finding what we are looking for, says Momo, as long as we are remaining friends says Chris and as long as I can breathe fresh air says Jo. All is fine and the ship takes off to the endless shores of discovery.
The wind is blowing, the waves are mild and peaceful and the three are looking forward for their first destination.

The shores of a never ending Discovery offer fresh air to breathe and more. The discovery brings the explorers closer to themselves. Let's breathe through with the seafarers and hope for good winds. As the wind allows one to be able to move, one sets sail with the help of the life air, we breathe - we live.

Breathe and come along a journey where we explore the beauty of the breath. Can you hear it? It is with us. Inhale, Exhale. Can you hear the wind coming in and going out again? Can you feel the intensity of the air? The fresh, cool air, it allows us to live and explore. We can be in harmony with all. All is breathing and alive. Let's embrace that and follow the flow.

The friends are now in the middle of the vast sea and there we spot the first great discovery. It must be an animal as large as the vessel, it splashed a fin and a high fountain of water rises into the air, as it seems to be breathing, we might find a friend in this being. This being has a long tail, like a giant fish and it has black skin and a white belly, as well as a large mouth. Luckily it seems to play and have fun. The fin splashes again into the water and a large water tower elevates into the air.

The water is the great connection.

I am water, you are water, we are all connected with the water. The water is us. One is with the soothing balance, the harmony and unity, as we are all on the same sea. Let's sea and find how the water giant is doing. Chris calls out: Hey, big friend, are you okay? We can help you we are here on the sea. Let's unite together in harmony, as we are all part of the water. Let's find a way.

I am the protector of the Underwater City, and My name is Elias the White Humpback Whale. I am the benefactor or all under water creatures and I am glad to meet you, because I heard you like to save and protect the precious stories of the water world.

This is your chance to have a meeting with my friends just follow me.

We can believe this wonderful incident, this beautiful and giant creature just

invited us for a water party, well, the three sailors are more than happy, and yes we are here to protect and connect for experience. As we gain experience we can live a life of peace and trust.
Let's breathe in deeply, and follow Elias tor a new discovery.

Just see, we whales are only feeding of what's already in the sea, oh there is Lizy and there is Josiah, my brother and sister, we are vegetarians and have always been. As we are famous for our songs, we like to introduce you to hump back whale singing.
The three giant whales open their mouths and a sonar of water sounds comes clear to our ears, unique in nature, the three add melodies and harmonies to their choir which soothes even the toughest seafarer.

Follow the whales,
Into the waves,
Hear their song
And forget all along,
All craving and desire,

The will to aspire,
Crystal clear sapphire,
Beautiful like water and fire.

Let's hear the rhythm of the sea,
See, one can feel the harmony.
Let the whales show you how to be,
In Peace, Love and Unity.

The endless waves of bliss touch the hearts of the three seafarers and the endless curiosity became still for a moment. The moment of the whale song remains back on board. What a masterpiece! With a big gasp of fresh air the three come back to their journey, but how can one be so Gigantic just by eating greens?

Anyway the wind never stops
And blows the three towards the wide sea where now Dolphins play around the vessel shaking their heads in an asking manner, what is it that you are looking for, come we have a treasure, right below, the three just wink and say: Hey, we are safe here on board, but you are

smart enough to know, that we have all the treasures with us and our stories.
The Dolphins laugh and one starts to sing a Dolphin song.

Three seafarers look for new hope and land, otherwise we could not give you a hand, because we only have fins, and a blow hole, see the water coming out of the whole!

The dolphins blow a nice water fountain out of their blow hole and the three sailors get a large dolphin shower, but they start to laugh and that's normal on the sea, you might get wet by a dolphin who likes to play.

Even further down the sea the three come to make the next discovery, close to an island, not so far away, there is a wise turtle with a soothing grin and a whole family on its back.
All the turtles seem to be so content and kind around this wise and old turtle. There is an aura of peace surrounding

this family and the three explorers become very warm-hearted.
This is what we are looking for, away from home we have collected all these stories, but what is the first chapter of ones life? It is the raise from a baby to a child, the wonderful journey from the first steps to the first words, the first school visit and the first date.

All we are doing now is leaving it behind, even though we can be in between.
Let's breathe once more this wonderful fresh air of the wide and free world of liberty and remain with this sight of the peaceful turtle and its family.

The turtle smiles and the three are on a way home for good, knowing their mothers and fathers, brothers and sisters, Uncles and aunts, as well as all the friends are waiting. Now they have beautiful stories of the whales, the giant protectors of the sea, the dolphins that love to play and blow water from a hole and the most lovely turtle, so old and wise, taking care of all the family.

In serenity all the ocean and sea needs to be safe and protected, all three agree, it is a previous gem of lives that come to live like us, in peace and with family. All the lives matter in this vast world, as the three come home, all have gathered to hear a bit of their journeys, yet the travelers are just happy to be embraced and to have the same old feeling of home again.

Coming home is like coming to rest, to ones own body, which we fully know and trust. Know the breath and one shall know the waves, and tides, of the endless ocean of discovery. Life is a wonderful journey, as we breathe, as we relax into the good good night.

Dream on the vast ocean of possibility, rest, relax and sleep well.

Whale Story

<u>1483 words, 20 minutes</u>

This is the story of Elias the Whale, a white humpback whale who grows up in the vast ocean near the shores of a continent we know as Australia. Elias knows all the ocean around this island continent and is content to be with his family. His sister Lizzie and his brother Josiah are equally a humpback whale living as a happy family In the ocean. All of them are vegetarian, as they only eat the green plankton which they find in the sea. As Elias is now together with his family they swim to another vacation destination.

They want to make holiday on the beautiful shores of the Gold Coast. This is where people are very friendly out to the white whales: Elias loves the people and when he sees one on the boat or on the shore he splashes with his fin a huge water tower into the air. So one can see that there is a whale. Wow look at this whale! Elias and his family are also well known for that song, as whales are beautiful singers. It is like a long tone from the mouth of the whale that vibrates for hundreds of Kilometers in the ocean and other whales can hear it even very far away. This is how whales communicate.

A whale sound goes like that, AWUHUWAAA.
He is a fish in the sea, a very large and precious one. One day Elias will become the father of a family who is the single singer of the orchestra. Hearing this song one might know that he is Elias the whale with a beautiful show. Everyone is unique, with the unique voice to show. Elias is the one to make the people happy.

Now let's breathe deeply and imagine we are on the vast ocean of the sea, to see that there is a splash in the distance, this must be Elias! On the Gold Coast with the chance to come close to Elias and his family, the whale gives us a show blowing a huge water fountain from his blow hole, singing and playing.

One can be mesmerized by this sight, as the sun shines bright the whales are also very wise, growing up to 15 metres long just by eating greens. This is how important it is to stay healthy and fit. Elias also moves a lot swimming many kilometres in the ocean every day, isn't that fascinating? Let's dive and swim with the Whale.

Imagine there's a protective bubble around you. We are breathing in this protective bubble, it is our protection to go under the sea. We are noticing the breath, how the breath is coming into the nostrils and going out again. The breath is always the central life force, so always keep track. Let's embrace the protection and come back to the underwater world where Elias lives.

Come along to our home, Elias is very excited that we are here with him and hopes he can make a good impression so we know how whales live under the sea. Essentially they don't have a TV or Sofa, they rest while gliding on a wave, just closing their eyes for a moment and knowing everything will be fine. The water shall carry one away. Into the nice and soothing dreams of a whale we find ourselves in midst the beautiful underwater world, where the water is crystal clear and wild. The waves are sometimes bigger than buildings but now the waves are calm and tranquil. Watch the waves of the ocean coming and going out again. The beautiful synchronicity of the wind and of the waves is the matter that moves the world.

Elias knows everything about the waves, but he knows only so little about the winds. However Elias knows the breath, even under water he can breathe and find balance in the breathing. He is fully aware of the movement, because the water is never still, here in the ocean there is always movement and dynamism. The wonderful thing is, Elias also loves to travel, together with his family he can use the movement to travel wherever he likes.

The family around Elias loves to travel too so they travel from the Gold Coast to the beautiful Shores of the Silver Coast. Here there are many fish living and there is also the families teacher living. He showed the family all about the surrounding of people and how to interact with humans. Elias was one of his best students. The sea is also full of interesting caves and ship wracks where sometimes divers come, to explore the wide variety in colourful fish. Yes, the ocean really is a stunning place for discovery:

So many whales that live here happily and free,
Wild it is but there is serenity.
All whales come along very well,
There is no harm as all are well and wise
What a surprise the sound of a whale,
Soothing and bright in nature
Announces a happy birthday,
Elias the underwater giant,

Knowing the people so well,
Is now celebrated with a special shell.
It makes a sound that is nice and loud,
Elias happily splashes and brings the water out,
From his blow hole the water shoots into the air.
Happy and joyful whales celebrate together,
Always moving with the water flow,
Gladly we are the ones to know,
How the whales come together in peace and unity.
May All beings live together in serenity.
Like the ocean all beings shall be protected,
And kept pure and clean, like the water crystal clear.
We are here, breathing underwater in a protective bubble just exploring and finding a new way, in midst the underwater trees and plants, shining in beautiful colours we glance. Thanks to Elias showing us the wide world of the ocean, bringing us closer to the shore, Elias helps us and we can hop on the

whales back, which has a bump , that's why humpback whale.

Riding on the whales back we travel through the sea, knowing the protecting and security we hold on very well, so we keep the balance of the travel way. Where would one like to go on a back of the whale? Maybe to a safe haven or shore, maybe into the night, we are finding a nice sunset spot, alright.

From the waters the glitter of the sun, intense and bright, shimmers on the surface of the incoming night: The colours shift, the night comes in, in peace we cheer the sight, a golden ball sets into the sea, we find there is a tomorrow and there might be eternity. As the waves are coming and going, rising and passing away, everything is here to sway, up and down, from left to right and back, into the night. Let's celebrate the sight and one might find that everything is alright. The whales are sounding their favourite tunes.

Thank you world for the light, and for the night,
We love the ocean, we love the sea,
Everything is a small part of thee, whole, harmony.

Together we find family and the peace and serenity.
Like the waves come to shore, we come to ease,
Let's find serenity and peace.
May All beings under and over water be safe and sound,
May all beings be happy even to the deepest ground,
May all beings be helped and found,
Safe, and serene and sound.

All is good and we gently see the first stars in the sky, the moon appears likewise; too.
By the energy of the sun and moon, the tides come and go, by the power of the breath our life comes and goes. Let's breathe in peace and serenity and let's go for a good night.

We breathe into a good night and we let go for a goodbye. Breathing in and out. Thanks and all the appreciation for Elias and the whale family, as well as to all the whale family. All appreciation to the protectors of the sea, let's keep it pure and clean. The power of the ocean is with its inhabitants, as the ocean is just a part of earth, we are all here to keep and maintain the peace and serenity.

Elias also gives thanks with a beautiful whale sound: AWUHUWAAA and splashes once more giant masses of good night water into the star-sprinkled air. The light of the moon cools the senses and Elias dives back into the deep traveling ocean to maybe one day come close to you again, but until we can dream to swim with the whales and we can keep the connection with our breath, as all the beings are connected with the breath, with the water, the light.

Let's all be happy and content in this peaceful night,
Let's all share the way to be alright,

Let's all embrace the light,
Even in the good good night,
Sleep well and rest alright.

Dolphin story

<u>1503 words, 20 minutes</u>

Once upon a time there lived playful dolphins in the wide, wide ocean. They were so playful, they were even considered playful dolphins, but no zoo nor any man could ever keep them, they were so playful, they remained In wild freedom.

The freedom of the dolphin, is to be active and to roam around on the waves and in the ocean. As a dolphin plays it sometimes forgets the time and space and it can even become night and the dolphin would not know. Yet the dolphins are very intelligent and they know all the games of the underwater animals. Sometimes even Sharks, they were so smart, that they were outplayed by the dolphins as the Dolphins are just so clever communicating that no single animal has a chance.

It is the radiant sound of a dolphin that makes it noticeably beautiful, sometimes so beautiful other sea animals like sharks just fall in love with the dolphins, as the dolphins all look alike, they bring another dolphin to play and hence one can not decide which one is the more beautiful. This works every time. Also dolphins are very attentive to playmates and friends, they celebrate every day as friends day and therefore show their affection by singing or even touching nose to nose.

This is a sign of a lovely devotion towards one another. The affection is also expressed by laughing and smiling, because after a long day of swimming and playing, the dolphins are very tired, however they can relax best while laughing and singing soothing songs.

Under the sea, we are happy, laughing and cheering the Day,
We are always happy, as we have friends and family.

The sea is our home and we play our favourite songs each and every day, we feel alright and okay by the vast ocean grace, we also sometimes see a human face and when we do we laugh so much, that water springs from our blow hole and shoots out into the air.
Ha ha ha Ho Ho Ho Hu hu hu Hey hey hey hi hi hi.
Our love is all in care in the vast waters to sing and dance, yes we laugh and dance a lot and therefore praise the life. It is beautiful to be alive!

The dolphins jump out of the water to splash with a belly flap, and water rises into the air, sometimes so gracefully, we see the over water world. We like to jump and grow as friends, over the water we know there are no ends to the sky, the humans and beings alike, but we are dolphins the graceful beauty of the sea, swimming, singing and laughing in harmony. That might be, our destiny.

We come to explore the wide worlds of the blessed sea life, which never retires

or stands still, always moving with the.wind, the waves come and go, and as well as one asks the dolphins to teach, how to be so gracefully in harmony with the sea.
Please dear dolphins, so magical and wild, how come you have the world of the waters so beautifully discovered and within? How do live so well with that?

You mean the fin? This like the legs you have and one can walk, but I am born deep in the sea and therefore we are here, and meant to be, a fin that moves up and down, left and right, is to navigate and feel, alright?

We are naval animals and long to be forever content with the waters, but you, it's all about being happy and at peace. Wherever we find ease. Our parents were the heirs of the sea and therefore we live here since we can see. So we just follow our parents and way to be happy. We also can breathe and therefore we are beings like you, living on this earth together with the water and the sun, with the light and the night.

We are dancing till the night, having to feel alive.
You are well invited to come with us, to see us dance and joyfully sing our playful chants.
Tonight there is a dolphin wedding and we celebrate the relationship of our dearest friend and singer, Sachran; the ever-funny and beautiful dolphin will be uniting with the dearest Sachruy who loves to be a dancing dolphin. One day they will show everyone how beautiful life of the underwater sea is. Hence they are practicing the art of underwater dance for their whole lives. They are inspired by their brothers and sisters who are all coming together to celebrate this wedding.

So come along to see the dolphin wedding harmony. The harmony starts with the big choir of many fishes and whales, as well as merman and mermaids who are likely to play the harps, under water shells and other musical sea instruments. There are underwater balloons and many visitors come from across the sea. Do you know this is the place of the wedding. Yeah, this wedding takes place! Let's dive in.

All the animals join together, to witness two dolphins unite and playfully have a reason to celebrate. Dolphins love to celebrate but even on a big wedding there is much going on, there are dolphins bringing underwater cakes, there are dolphins making underwater arts and craft for the kids, there is an underwater light show, and of coarse the choir is playing underwater music for everyone. As the bride is ready, cool drinks are handed to everyone, and the husband is speaking a toast to all the dolphin family.

I am glad, that we all can come here in peace and harmony, celebrating this unity. It is my wish and my blessing, that the whole ocean family comes together as one, to protect and playfully safe the ocean. The ocean is our greatest gift and we are so happy to have it. The ocean is like a big mother to us, and the earth is like the father that holds the ocean. We are all children of this world, and the only reason we are here, is because of our parents. So let's thank our parents. Let's all have a good time, and embrace the waters, playfully dancing, chanting, and being in harmony.

One can see, with the dolphins we have a good example of animals and a part of our earth. We all just want to live in harmony, yet we are acting differently, let's be aware of what we do and how one celebrates.

The dolphin party goes deep into the night, and everybody is sharing the site, happily uniting husband and bride swimming next to each other, in full sight. The party comes in full swing and beautifully the loved-ones are now to close the night with a last dance.

The last dance of the dolphins, only for this night, because they're dancing lights, will even shine into more nights. As the Waves come and go home, the shore remains the same, so the dolphin will ever be the best at this game in the sea, so come on, play fully, enjoying the waters in the sea, so beautifully, having always a reason to celebrate for life and for eternity.

Let's find out, how are the Dolphins are enjoying a good rest. As said, the dolphins like to laugh to relax, so let's try this. Ha ha ha, ho ho ho, hey hey hey, let the belly bounce. Just try your best to laugh like a dolphin, Ha ha ha, ho ho ho, hey hey hey, just feel the belly and laugh as loud as you can, don't worry about the neighbours, as laughing is the best remedy for relief, it is also good night medicine.

Just imagine the dolphins all together swimming into the night, under the nice moonlight, see them dancing and smiling, and just smile yourself. Be kind, and happy, with yourself, your parents and all around you. Remember the toast of the dolphin saying we are all one, every single one is a part of this earth? So how we live is key, and one might be as happy, joyfully and in harmony like the dolphins. Under the same moon, under the same light, may this be a blessed night.

Surround yourself with a crystal clear light and hear the sounds of the ocean, maybe one even hears the laughing of the dolphins, singing us a joyful song, relax and find ease with every single breath. Deeper and deeper we sink into the world of dreams where we are happily joined in protection and safe sound, by the voice and the ambient of the night.

There always is a light, even in the darkest night, one might be this, oh so bright, shining into the night, with a simple smile we can enlighten, even the darkest sea, with a smile, one might be able to see, what is peace, what is love, what is harmony.
Rest and relax for a good night.

Underwater Story

<u>1479 words, 20 minutes</u>

Once upon a time there was an underwater kingdom with a king and a queen. The kingdom was build next to an ocean, when a phenomenal earthquake happened and the city sunk into the depths of the ocean, this city is now inhabited by queen Zoronia and king Yuddha which are both native to the water. Like every good kingdom the queen and king loved to have celebrations, this time due to the birth of their first daughter which presented the kingdoms heritage. Down in the underwater city, the kingdom was part of an even larger kingdom under the guidance of Neptune, the King of the whole ocean.

When Neptune heard of the birth he was very delighted and sent his best guides to travel with him to the faraway underwater kingdom. The celebration shall takes place in the community square, where all the inhabitants of the small kingdom gathered. The dolphins brought themselves and some dolphin cake, the whales got their finest songs and the mermaids, as well as merman got themselves musical instruments to celebrate the new birth. Queen and King are happily joined by all the family members from the vast ocean family.

Underwater flowers are decorating the pathways and garlands of beautiful sea stars are given to the guests. Feel welcome and celebrate with us, it is a great day. There is also the King of the Ocean coming to celebrate with us. Many wonderful beings join around Neptune when he arrives and there he presents his birthday gift for the young one. It is a tiny conch shell for future music.

The priest are blowing this conch shell for procession and the whole ocean vibrates with joy and serenity. Even the turtles and little children turtles are there, even the oldest and wisest one.

The young and old, the wise and not so wise, the far and close ones all can celebrate together and the kingdom also knows to invite some people, like us, to their party as it is a beautiful spectacle they are sure, we like to see it, too.

Imagine crystal clear waters and an ancient underwater city that is alive and coloured in the most magnificent splendour, drenched in tastes and scents. All are welcome to join, and maybe we like to bring a friend to this celebration with us.
This is the chance to also think about a gift, what would we present, maybe a message, or maybe a happy birthday song.

Happy birthday to the princess of the underwater world. It's a beautiful appearance and the whole ocean is there to see the festivity.
The Queen and King are also happy, just sitting in the throne having a smile onto everyone. The birth of a newborn is

always a delight and the baby is fully protected in a nice basket of gold and wool, safely slumbering.

We can imagine all the celebration just for one person, but the celebration is always on, as underwater creatures love to party and come together. Yet, we can imagine, it is probably the wide range and space in the ocean that makes it possible. Some kingdoms in the underwater world reach down to 10000, ten thousand metres, and these kingdoms are rarely visible, because in the depth there is pure darkness. Yet, there are still kings and queens living down there, and one of them is even coming to this celebration.

One may see, in the depth of the ocean, there is pure serenity, no stress, no tension, just watery peace, a gentle reminder of who we are - Peace.
The depth and darkness are one of a kind, yet this underwater kingdom shines with light. It is close to the shore

in the Meditational sea, where bliss is essence and happiness to be.

We can dive into this sea and see it ourselves, the tranquility and peace are one of a kind. So prepare yourself with a breath and relax, because the more we relax, the deeper we dive. Into the ocean there are many mysteries unsolved, yet the place is safe and sound, with a guide, like Neptune, we can truly explore, breathing deeper and deeper, to the kingdoms door.

The entrance is clear and open for us to come, this is where the underwater journey has begun, a mermen is waiting for us to enter and we come in. It is a truly wonderful square, so vast and alive, well cared for and good, this is way to the Palast where the king and queen reside, just celebrating in full delight.

There is always reason to take it slow, with every breath we are the ones to know, breathing is light, even underwater we can, imagine, imagine, imagine.

Imagine all the fishes, living in this world,
Underwater, happy for today,
And tomorrow there shall be peace in every way.

Imagine all the colours, of the mermaids, dolphins and whales and there even is a fountain in the middle of the square bringing forth beautiful water bubbles of multicoloured goodness. Everything here seems so tender and soft, the waters are an element of balance. Even overcoming the biggest gap, water can reach everywhere without a miss. Even reaching the tops of the world, water disguised in snow can be every on this world.

In the air, under the Earth, in the Forest, and the sea,
Water is within and with us, to be.
We are waters as everyone is water, likewise connected with the elemental flow, springing from a source, growing

up in water, rising to be born and living a life. The waters are ceaseless and always in flux, eternally adaptive and making us alive.

We can speak to the water and it listens to us, it is brave and tender at the same time. Water, is alive and always in flow, may give to understand, waters also know.
Knowing the form and shapes of life, we can see that water is always here for balance and harmony.

In the Kingdom all are in Balance and harmony, within, waters make a way, we can be thankful for each and every day. Let's praise the water and give thanks for its delight, also when there comes a good night. Water adjusts and reflects what is there, light of the moon shimmers and the water is in care.
This is life, and life is water. Water is life and thankful we can be. Appreciate every drop and in abundance it may show, water springs, and comes in a flow. The waters are here to heal and

nurture our growth, may one be fostered and held with life.

Thank you water, for making us feel alive, even in the good, good night.

We arrive at the kings throne to see the newborn and the queen are equally happy to see us. We are smiling in gratitude and hopefully we have a glimpse. Though we can see, a question arises in ourselves. What can I do to protect? Protect the water, as the water protects itself, protect yourself and the water is protected. The king smiles and adds, and maybe drink hot water in the morning, to start a good day, sometimes one can add some honey.
This recipe is by my grandma, the king gives us a wink and grins, let's celebrate the night under the moon light.

To say the least, the underwater life is magical, yet the parties are even more magnificent and we are helping us to a wonderful seat, where we can watch and witness the harmony, of the dolphins dancing with smily faces, the whales singing their ear-full songs, the merman are waving their flutes and harps, playing the melodies of joy and peace, and mermaids are bringing flowers to make everything look nice. What a surprise Neptune holds a speech:

May all water creatures live in harmony with thee, may all beings appreciate the waters we have and live in unity.

Let's celebrate this kingdom and welcome all our guests, that are coming here for a new quest. The quest is to protect and maintain, the precious, subtle and clear waters of the earth. By celebrating we hope to endure and praise the everlasting flow of life, that may rise and go, all the waters may rise and go, so does the night rise, and we shall have a good rest, so we are prepared to protect, with the help of the breath, we are here to live.

Let's live All in Peace, Love and Unity.

Let's also enjoy this scene and give our personal appreciation for what we have seen.

It has now been the chance to have a good night and further show our light, with a sincere smile we illuminate the night. May the stars twinkle, the moon beam and we find the peace, resting and relaxing, wholly, into the night.
Sleep well.

Rainbow story

<u>1635 words, 25 minutes</u>

Imagine a land of many possibilities, right away, but here for you to be. The place I am speaking of is in your imagination and here one can find endless worlds to discover. So, let's go for a walk and find a comfortable position to relax the body. Is the body relaxed, the mind and the imagination can blossom like a beautiful flower. This flower of the Self is within everyone's reach and can be attained by everyone. It is our human possibility, like a smile one can make people smile, too.

In this world we have the power to dream of anything possible, so let's relax the body and envision a wonderful world. Be aware of the breathing, while you are relaxing the head, this may give steadiness and grace to your being. Relax the body and breathe. The breathing is equally coming in and going out again. It is in one harmonious flow.

The in-breath is our dear friend and the out-breath is our dear friend leaving us for a moment. Let's embrace this friend. Hello, welcome dear Breath, and Goodbye, dear Breath it is nice meeting you. The breath is always with us, saying hello for the space we are in and entering into the nostrils, streaming into the body. Within the body our friend enters our bodily kingdom.

It makes connection with our lungs, heart and other friends. The incoming breath is very well invited to also meet the belly. The belly is our common friend. Everyone knows the belly, as the friends meet together at the belly button, all the friends equally find themselves traveling back and forth, so the in-coming friend, the breath, now is saying hello to everyone, meeting and greeting the other friends, like the heart, the lungs, the belly, but also the cells and mitochondrion, as the breath can travel everywhere we can also meet the toes with the breath.

So the friends, aka tippy toe and the breath meet, greet and have a connection. This connection is very fragile and soft, so come, it can be even just spontaneous. When these meetings are done, the wonderful friendship parts and the beautiful journey goes on. So the breath says goodbye, I will see you, and then travels back from the lungs, over the nostrils into the space again: where we call this exhale. In the Space the breath is free to be.

From here, we are noticing the friendship and we are aware of the breath and with every single breath one can relax, or energize. However one likes. Now, as the we like to focus on the imagination, we just relax the body, so we are sure, not to float away. Balanced and safe we are grounded and relaxed, with the breath. The breathing goes in and comes out again, and we notice that the inhale is equal to the exhale, just fine and balanced.

The balance spreads around the whole body and we become lighter and lighter. We are becoming so light, we start to sink into our wonderful world of imagination where we can sit in a garden of friendship. This Garden of Friendship is free for us to be. We can invite all our friends or we can just sit in serenity. There is a nice cushioned grass patch for us, it is very soft and really inviting us for a meditation.

So we are sitting here, meditating with our bottom on the ground and we feel the soft grass on this lush field, there is also a tree, and we see, the tree greets us, too. Hello tree and beautifully the tree gives us shelter and a steady help to maintain peaceful and calm, this is what trees do, staying peaceful and calm. Beautiful isn't it? The tree is obliged and greets us with a smile, we smile back.

We are all breathing the same air, and look up into the air, there was just a fresh rain shower and now the sun comes along again, what a wonderful surprise the moisture in the air and over the field creates a haze where the sun shines through and there we have a glimpse of a multicoloured rainbow, shining and bowing to us, oh Hello, dear friend, I am the Rainbow; Welcome!

The rainbow bows at our feet and we are just seeing a lovely rainbow, that invites us with many beautiful colours, tender red, and golden orange, shiny yellow, bright green, light blue, indigo, and violett. All the colours are now with us, greeting us one by one, always bowing and Saying, Hello I am indigo, Hello, I am golden Orange, Hello, I am bright Green; and everyone smiles and we smile back.

The rainbow welcomes us for a walk and we can walk with the rainbow to see, where does this rainbow come from, yes, we Can show you. I am coming from the source. I am a rainbow born from the light, and born from the wonderful world. Here in this world you only see my seven colours, but in the imaginary world, the spiritual plane, the world is endlessly filled with abundant colours. There is no limit to the colours, as long as you can imagine you can also envision them. The colours I show you are within you right now, says the rainbow, and are coming out from this source.

We are standing on the side of an infinite pool, opening many beautiful layers of colours, it is a fountain, that springs with facets, oh friends, have you ever seen? This is the source of the rainbow, and it is beautiful.

The source seems to never end, and always creates itself from new. As soon as we think of a colour; indigo, indigo, indigo, the fountain becomes alive with this colour and we can also imagine forms, balls, flows, triangles and the fountain gives out many forms and shapes. It is a vision of the imagination, the eyes are ready to receive a wonderful gift of the mind. In our material world, the physical plane, only so much colours can be perceived, but within the dreamy, imaginary world, there is space to also free ourselves into more space. Space means the possibility to perceive more than meets the eye.

Oh, let's wonder why, the rainbow is coloured like it is,
anyway, the source is a source of bliss,
It springs endlessly coming into life, full of happiness.
The divine nature, the rainbow and the discovery is what it is.

Let's invite a friend to come with us on this imaginary world discovery, where everything is possible and let's say: thank you to the rainbow and the tree. What a wonderful harmony, this can be. Imagine yourself with the dearest of your friends, and invite this friend dearly; like the breath. One shall come and enjoy the imaginary paradise, as well as the gardens of friendship.

 For a walk into the night, one can make it feel alright. Let's again envision the forms and shapes and know this is all here to be, our friend is now with thee. See, your dearest friend, heartily and kind, smiling, appreciating this friendship. Let's embrace this friend with all the colours of the rainbow. With all the love and devotion, with all the happiness and joy. Let's smile and find ourselves guided by the light, even in the darkest night.

Let's remember once more the beautiful discovery in this garden of friendship and how all the beings can be friends, peaceful and calm like the tree, in colourful serenity, the tender red, golden orange; shiny yellow, bright green, light blue; indigo and violet: all are here for friendship and for life, like the breath, making one feel alive. All the parts of the body are now in connection, in peace and serenity. There is now wholesome balance and harmony, from the tippy toes to the head, as are full in rest.

May All the beings be happy and free, in the colourful world of harmony,

May my friendship be with all, all the beings may be friends,
May the love and peace surround the whole world for good life.

May there always be light, even in the darkest night,
May our happiness and joy shine bright even in the darkest night,
May we greet the moon and the stars with a smile,
May ones happiness last for a while:
May all the beings be safe and sound, in peace, in love and harmony.
May I come back to the breath and to the body,
To fully engage in the life right here, right now. Chant and be happy.

I am the light of the world:
I am the light of the world;
I am, I am; I am the light of the world.

You are the light of this world,
You are the light of this world;
you are; you are; you are the light of this world.

We are the light of this world, we are the light of this world, we are we are, we are the light of this world.

May all be friends; may all be the light, even in the darkest night.

Parents Story

<u>1460 words, 20 minutes</u>

Once upon a time there was a family, that lives in the forest by the river stream. It is a sacred valley in midst the hills, where the family has a small lot for their cows and crops.
The family is a large family with 6 children, 3 boys and 3 girls. The peace of the lot is due to its nature, growing up on a land that is very safe and sound. The parents of the family are quite happy. As the work is benefitting, the nature is kind,u the crops are growing and the cows are giving milk. Around the lot there is a large forest and after the work is done the family enjoys together at the nearby stream. Cool and fresh water is running from its source just steps away, hidden in the forest.

The forest is a sacred one and the trees are as old as the family tree. When the young children come back from playing in the forest they enjoy a soothing

evening with all the family members reading stories and playing music. The father of the family is the one who holds dear a very thick book, layered in leather. This book holds all the stories from the family as well as memories. In this thick book called the family tree book, all the leaves are filled with stories and every single evening, one is ready to read, a new story.
The father begins to tell the story of himself as a cowherd boy who gently and mildly plays the flute to soften the cows.

As the cows are grazing, the sound of the flute is also attracting the cowherd girls who are very tender and soft-skinned. They are maidens of the barn and equally share their work, bringing milk from the cows to the village where everyone shares the milk.

As one day I was playing my flute, says the father in a light voice, the cowherd girls came around to witness the scene seeing the cows joining in for a MOO and they start to laugh, one of them, even came to me, listening very closely. Attentively she looks at me, and there I knew, love is like a spontaneous flash that travels through all my veins and I became so devotionally encircled, to play the most beautiful melodies

.

The father looks over his reading glasses into the eyes of the children, like he always does, and there he sees the first member of the family already falling asleep. He smiles and continues in the book and reads on. This is how I got to meet your Mother, in this old memory I still find my love for her, and the love for the music remains.

Playing music is like embracing all the beings, because sometimes when Mother listens so kindly, the cows started to be amused with envy, they moo'd so loud that I didn't hear a word, but that just showed me, they feel for me, too.

Of course Mother was still so very young and we were rather happy to roam around the forest and play with each other, dancing and singing with the birds. While I was hiding in the tree I witnessed the wonderful cow maidens washing their clothes in the river just here and when they were bathing inside the river, I was sneaking down, hiding the clothes in the trees. When the maidens came out, they were in wonder where in the world would these washed clothes go? They could not walk from alone, but as I am a gentle soul, I gave them hints with my flute. Playing and making sounds to guide them into the forest to let them seek the clothes, of course I did not make any play with your Mother, because she knew who was playing the flute and was not in wonder.

Sitting up in the trees she glimpsed at me and I fell into her hands, she then got me and pushed me into the group of maidens who all saw me with my flute, I could not help myself, instead to play a song for them all and surely so sweet and tender they all forgave me. This song I still remember to this day.

Your Mother and I, we became very deep friends and sooner or later she met me alone, on a cool summer night, we were just sitting in the swing, swinging up and down enjoying the moon light. It was all in private secrecy but we enjoyed the beautiful moment. In these moments I can spot every detail, even every breath and it makes one so happy, I love to tell you more. Looking over the glasses, the next child fell asleep, very soon the father answered with a smile. What a surprise, the story goes on and comes around with a lesson.

Having family is to trust oneself and the partner. It is to obey and follow, and also to serve in devotion and love. As we all loved to dance, we organized dance gatherings in the forest, just lit with the light of the moon, the community was always very happy to hear my flute and to come together. Everyone was dancing, swirling around in circles following the beat of the drum. The rhythm got us and we continued deep into the night, while we were wearing our most elegant dresses. The parties were without any intoxication, we were just in happiness by moving and dancing.

When I got to dance with Mother the spark ignited a sacred flame that burns until this day, it is the flame that tenderly warms me from the inside and helps when I feel cold. Even in the cool night, the movement to the rhythm, looking into Mothers eyes feels like a warm shower.
From the sky sometimes dropped rain in and we all had to hide somewhere, of course I was hiding the best and could smile when I found another hiding spot with her maiden friends, I ask them, come on and dance along in the rain.

The rain dance could not extinguish the flame of excitement and joy within me, dancing with Mother in the rain, so in love and devotion; to the rhythm of the beat of the drum. Always following the next great adventure, we got together finding a dry spot at our home; in a safe nest, with a warm oven, making some tea and enjoying the smells of incense and herbs.

We just hold on here and continue next time, the Father looks over the glasses and another one was sleeping already. Then sooner enough, Mother comes into the room with a warm milk and Father closes the Story book. It is about that life, coming to ease, listening to stories, dancing and finding harmony. Love is like the honey in the milk that gives it a special taste.

Tender and sweet it awakens our senses and one feels a sense of life. To be alive means to love, love means to live. Aliveness comes from the union of our beings, sometimes even in a dark night, we can smile and shine bright. All families are unique and one of a kind, this is why we shall thank and appreciate every moment to feel alive. The family is also like a tree, bringing flowers and

fruits to flourish and blossom. When the fruits are ripe and the flowers blossom they give us a special nectar, that when ready, is like honey, too. We are like bees enjoying this nectar and essentially bringing it back
Home into the Hive. Here the family resides and dances, and comes together in unity. Let's celebrate our harmony.

For once the family father pulls out his flute and plays a soothing good night lullaby, as Mother sings her favourite phrases from a book:

Like a light that stands still in the wind, the one who listens to the music of the mind, meditates and finds the ease, please,
Bring us harmony and peace, please bring us harmony and ease.
Together we are meditating and doing our deeds, raising a family, planting a tree, creating a life and living in harmony. Whatever comes, whatever goes, one is steady in action and mind,

Let's unwind into a good, good night.

The play softens and fades, the family shuts the lights, yet is happy in harmony into the star-sprinkled night.

Let's find relaxation in every breath and continue to equally relax the body,
While breathing in and out, equally the rhythm of the breath goes.
We just follow along in the everlasting song, of life and light.
Following with a peaceful rest and a balanced state of mind.
Sleep, rest and relax.

Turtle Story

<u>1486 words, 20 minutes</u>

There once lived a wonderful Turtle named Kurma, Kurma the Turtle, is a wise and wonderful being that lives together in peace and harmony with its family. Kurma one day swims in the vast ocean of experiences to gather a glance if everything is alright. In the ocean of experiences it sometimes happens that there is a fight, and Kurma the wise turtle knows to bring long-lasting peace into the waters.

And there we go, two crabs are in a harsh discussion who is the harder shell, and eventually Kurma bears to wait until the long discussion ends, yet Kurma has much time and patience. The crabs, are now just wondering what is this wise turtle doing here. Is it listening to us? Kurma smiles and yes, Kurma listens and knows you two have an argument that ends no where, as eventually one or even two of you might be graced to be a nice conch shell for Neptune's orchestra. The Turtle smiles and sees the crabs in wonder. Neptune? Conch Shell? Who are you!

I am Kurma, to bring peace and long-lasting harmony into the waters and all life matters to me, it matters to me, because we have all the responsibility to keep the waters safe. The sound of Kurma soothes the crabs. Who is fighting who is harder is not relevant as all shall pass, and the ocean will maybe leave some sand behind, even the wisest and oldest turtle knows that. The crabs are baffled and start to ask, so please, wise turtle, what is the meaning of life? Kurma knows to be a happy helper and suggests to find it out themselves, yet he knows what is it not:

Either Hard, nor Bold, whether strong, nor stark,
All shall pass with a happy spark,
As a drop falls into the ocean,
We are all here just a moment in time,
We are like a breath, coming to go.

As the waters flow, fleeting in life.
Our only meaning is to be alive.
What does it matter, let's enjoy the time, to live a life, to ignite and spark the night. Every being is illuminating by a breath. Let's come together and celebrate. Kurma knows the crabs are wonderful musicians playing the hand drums, yet they waste their lives in fight. Play and let's have a good time.

Kurma leaves the crabs and invites them for a good night party, celebrating the kingdom of the underwater sea. Neptune shall come to have a party, personally. The crabs are happy to enjoy, coming along for the party and a song.

Under the sea, we found the meaning of Life, thanks to a turtle so wise, let's live a life!
Let's live a life in serving, doing the best we can, to enjoy every moment.
The crabs are happily clapping their hands and cheering. Happy Days, ending the fights, coming on a way.

Of goodness and harmony the Turtle continues to seek out the seas and bringing peace to thee. Kurma never forgets his family and therefore first comes back home, where everyone is delighted to see, Kurma helped another day of peace in the sea. The Sea is sometimes wild and a pool of meaning and ground. This is why the waves are making such a sound. Kurma comes home and enjoys the waves of tranquility and serenity.

Here we are breathing with the turtles, swimming in the sea, let's find a vessel, and we are ready to dive deep, there is no discussion as the turtles know to turn anger into music, we all can be a part. Let's enjoy the goodness of the sound, anyway, we trust, breathing and trust. A protective shield around the body relaxes the Self, Kurma invites us to come home.

We are seeing the ancient turtle almost growing larger than a car, with precious fins and a smile that is of many worlds worth. The turtle knows the sea so well and comes to live a life in simplicity. What a surprise the wondrous sea allows for a guest like Neptune and thee. The party never stops as the waves come to shore, we are all here to adore.

Whoever has a question can come to Kurma for advise, so sometimes the king of the sea comes to help with thee, Kurma please, how can we solve all the worlds unease? Kurma thinks about the Kings question and extensively looks around. The wise Turtle sees no problem though it hears a sound, I am just a child of this sea, as we are all a big family. No one is better than others and no one is greater than another, no one is richer or more wise than others. Kurma admits, I am not wiser than you, only you yourself, can know what's true.

Inner truth comes from experience, by breathing we know.
The body, mind and soul all come together with the help of the breath, the

energy flows and can elevate all the sorrows of this world. We can be happy, we are alive, breathing and making a life. Let's embrace that. Let's not seek any fight, let's not seek any strive, all is alright, right here and now.
From afar a loud conch shell sound illuminates the talk. Kurma grins and knows it is time to celebrate the sun set. The king bows and comes to show his gratitude, you shall be on my side, while I am here. Come along, to sing our favourite song.

Kurma smiles and adds, only as I can bring my family. The king bows in gratitude and allows the whole family to come. Let's all dance and have fun. The little baby turtles are there, the smaller young turtles are there and the turtles are all sitting next to the king. The king is delighted and joined by the crabs who are playing their drums now in the orchestra. The whole underwater community joins around the square and this is where the mermaids and merman tone the conch shells again.

This sound of a deep: WUUUHHH invites all the Dolphins, Whales and friendly Sharks. They are all dancing with the songs of the drums, from left to right and right to left. In circles and up and down. The singing whales are giving a show and the Dolphins like to blow water from their holes. The sharks are continuing to dance and the others gaze and see, the whole water kingdom is in harmony.

The golden rays of the sun are beaming on the surface and the sky is turning into colours of splendour and grace, all are happy to lastly see the suns face. Kurma smiles and is happily surrounded by his family. He whispers to his children. Do you see, everyone is in synchronicity, following the rays of the sun, dancing To the beat of the drum, yet we are here and witness all that, do you see? This is what a king can be.

Seeing this world in peace, love and harmony is a dream and therefore can be real, all matter comes from the unknown worlds of mysteries. So splendid the sun shines all mysteries are dissolved and infused with light, as soon as it sets, the night reveals the dream. Every dream can come true, we just have to believe and trust the whole, the whole of us, is dreaming a collective dream, flowing in a constant stream.

One knows the rivers that spring from a source, life unfolds and the dream flows on and on and into the sea, where eventually, after long lives, comes to shore. This is the way of the water and the earth, feel obliged and blessed that one is here.

Into the night without a fear, let's all be kind and listen to what one says, even may it be the moon, shining our way, telling a story of far galaxy's and universes.

Just listen to the sound and hear your breathing coming in and out, listen in and one is found.

It all starts with a humble seed,

Listen and repeat, follow the wise,
Come to ease and find the wise in you.

Make it a deed and be fascinated by life,
Wonder what it is, always curious and in bliss.
Happiness is all around us, can you see?
Smile and be happy.

Kurma smiles and greets for a good night.
Let there be light even in the cool, dark night.
Let there be ease and peace, rest and serenity.
Let there be peace, love and harmony.

All equally, like the breath, in and out, coming and going, we are just breathing and happy to be alive, just happy to be alive. Relax yourself, fully breathing in and breathing out again. The breath comes and goes, and we ease with every single one.

Slower and finer, into the night, sleep well and rest.

Long life story

1492 words, 20 minutes

Once upon a time there was an eternal flame, burning for a long life. This flame was very well protected, guarded and kept safe. This flame was burning in the past and in the future, it is now present in every being. It is the everlasting flame of all love and of all life.
While we Breathe, This flame is transforming all the energies. As we breathe this fire is alive and flickering. To maintain this flame is to know the breath. This flame is sacred and also has a personality. It lives, flickers and dances in the wind, the wind is the everlasting play friend of the flame and the two are like best friends always finding a way of expressing themselves.

One is fully happy and in lust & laughter, that's the flame, one is harbouring the warm feelings of welcome home, that's the warm flickering flame of love and devotion. Flickering and dancing to the sounds of music, that's the joyful flame. All this is the same light, like the sun is equal to the sun light and the personality in the sun. The personality in the flame is called Agni, Devi or Goranga, shining in a golden bright light, the flame is always kept by the keepers. The keepers are also the keepers of wisdom who know the secrets of a long life.

Together we can all maintain our flame, and of course we can give our flame a personal name. The name of your flame might be different, yet it's one and the same. Like the rays of the sun is the same as the sun planet. Everyone can understand that.

Let's find this wonderful flame within our body and feel into it. It is very important to also know, that flames can transform a banana into a body. It is the flame that sparkles and sprinkles within our belly and it is the wonderful flame of digestion. This flame has many occupations, always busy and working tirelessly to

Maintain life.

So what does a flame need to steadily burn? Hm, it always needs a ground, because the flame has only so much space. So let's imagine a nice and beautiful space, like a shrine, an altar, maybe a safe fire pit, or even a tiny, tiny space as large as a candle light is also sacred and perfect for a flame. Agni doesn't matter how big the fire is, as long as it burns.
So, we close our eyes and imagine a wonderful flame within our dreamy world, in a sacred place. This place shall be totally serene and peaceful.

We can now sit by this sacred fire and find ourselves just knowing the guards are here to protect. A shimmer of golden light surrounds the sacred fire place. It heals, warms and nurtures our being and we find the fascinating sparkling of the flame speaking to us:

Oh Welcome to the inner fire that is here for you, I serve you as friend, fiery in

nature I am willing to make the best happen, I can also transform a banana into a body's fuel. Let's embrace this moment and thank each other for the meeting. As we breathe, we keep the fire alive, just breathe and keep the fire alive, alive and alive, with every single breath.
So, we sit at the fire place, and we breathe, it also smells of smoky wood and the scent is making us feel warm and nurtured.
The peaceful flame chants a song:

Like a candle in a place of serene shelter, where no winds blow, I am here to show that life is light, dancing into the night, nurturing the sight and making eyes bright.
I am to meditate with you, for a long life, letting one know, there is an easy way, one can practice every single day.

Let's meditate.

Inhale and Exhale, equally in and equally out again. See yourself in a sparkling shiny light, of devotion and love. See this light from the middle of you heart expanding into every cell of the body. This shimmering shiny light, shines from ones heart into every cell of the body. We become engrossed in shining light. We breathe and see ourselves in this light, just witnessing the beauty of it. The beauty of this light is in the heart, full of love and longevity.

Hold the breath in an equal rhythm, equally in, breathing through the nose and equally out again, letting the air go from the nostrils. The air streams into the body and helps inner life to move. The air is movement and with the breath the light can also move. The air travels with the light. See yourself protected with a beautiful glow, one is so safe and protected.

Now just keep the breathing equal and know everything is alright. The breath is moving in and out, the air constantly travels and we keep our senses to joy and happiness. Let's imagine a wonderful flame, the eternal flame of life, and we see it shine bright. Now let's invite a friend or family member to embrace this flame with us. It is a unique gift of life and we can share this present with the world and the loved ones around us.

When we breathe together, one can come into harmony. When we breathe under a tree, we come into harmony with that tree, when we come to breathe in synchronicity with a person, then we can come into harmony with that person. So let's unite with a friend or loved one and see that the breathing is nice and equal, harmonizing with the one.

Let's harmonize with all the world and see ourselves breathing life into the world. With every breath there is life streaming into the world, even the underwater beings and beings in the sky are breathing, somehow we are all connected with the air.

Let's celebrate this connection and find our friends and loved ones with us, so we can cheer the fire of celebration. The life flame dances and we sing songs of union. Let's pray and sing together.

Life is meant to be lived, dancing, chanting, in harmony.
Life is like a flame, playing in the wind, always enlightened,
Let the Light shine,
With a smile,
Let the love shine,
For a while,
Invite all you know,
Celebrate and show,
Affection and Love
The devotional flame dances and the sun goes down, but even in the darkest night, there, visibly shines a light. Light is also with us in our hands, the hands emanate healing light of love and therefore can heal. Our vision and eyes are connected to fire and the light, receiving and experiencing. Put your palms together in front of your heart, pray, and let a soft smile come onto your face. Now, run your palms together and see how the energy comes from the

palms of your hands, getting warm and energized the hands are now ready and fully loaded.

Open your palms and close your eyes. Put the warm hands onto the face, so they can enlighten ones eyes. Breathe into the warmth and hold still for a moment, witness the light streaming from your hands into the eyes and into the body again and again. Breathe, calmly in and out, equally, in and out. As we feel, just remain in balance, breathing and maybe trying it another time, maybe now one can open the eyes to even see the lights streaming from the hands into the eyes.

Let there be healing light flowing, this energy is just like a soft sun, inside our hands. The soft sun, shining from our hands finds a partner in the eyes who are receiving. There always needs to be a giver and one who receives. Let's now open the palms into the air, gently breathing and concentrating on the heart. Imagine a beautiful golden light in between hands and heart. From one hand to another, to the heart, there shines a healing light of longevity.

May this light be with me,
May this light be with you,
May this light be with all.
Repeat,

May this light be helping me,
May this light be helping you,
May this light be helping all.

Repeat,

May this light be truth
May this light be love,
May this light be peace.

Let's imagine this light streams with the breath, in and out, coming and going. Rising and passing, just like the breath comes there also comes the night, and even in the night we are breathing, light, feel alright and notice the soothing melody of the own breath, this is life.

Give thanks and appreciation to all the loved ones around you and find yourself happy, and smiling. Smile gently and give this smile to your friends and into the night. May this smile by the light. May All have a good night, let's feel alright,
Sleep, Rest, and Relax.

Fire Story

<u>1504 words, 20 minutes</u>

Once upon a time there was a wonderful kingdom, with a King named Orin and the kingdom was very beautiful and always lit, even in the night there were candles burning to illuminate the community square, the treasury and the kingdoms temple. Some people in the kingdom were even walking in the night along the paths that were lit with candles because it looks so beautiful.

This kingdom was a fire kingdom, there all the people and even children were wise with fire. It so was their work and life purpose to keep the fires of the world alive. Fire is not just a flame for them, but for the fire kingdom it means a sacred life, burning and transforming the energies of the here and now.

Fire gives warmth and light as it receives energy from the wood, or other materials. Therefore the fire kingdom

was also a wood forest, so they had enough to maintain the fire. In a beautiful setting by a stream, of crystal clear water, one might know that within the water is also a little bit of fire and vice verse. When you see a flame, there is also little shimmer of water in there, that's why water is necessary for fire.
Also all of the elements are connected with the wind or air.

So there was a visitor, he came from the air kingdom and the fire kingdom was very obliged to receive a guest, for tea. Heating water over the fire, the temple president of the fire kingdom receives the guest with joy, what a delight to see you here, it must have been a long journey from the high realm of the air kingdom. There are four air kingdoms, but there is only one fire kingdom, as the guest smiles he answers, it is always a pleasure to visit you and see if everything is alright, any fight or stress lately?

The temple president of the fire kingdom looks around, just the usual, we have now a better treatment for unhealthy fights and struggles, we let them play drums and other musical instruments to relieve the tension, you might be able to see them, as there is a parade on this occasion to celebrate the birthday of the kings daughter.
Everything is set with a nice walking orchestra, across the city and you are well invited to join the ceremony.

When the tea was ready the temple president takes a sip and smiles, ah, this tea is a remedy for anger and lust, it helps to digest and makes you easy to rest. What is it asks the air man, it just a cup of love, filled with herbs from the garden, I shall show you.

What we can do make the inner fire smooth is to let loose and enjoy a moment with a friend, let's breathe and relax, let's smile and meditate in the garden of the fire kingdom. We walk along the path where sacred lamps light the way, flowers are standing here and there, bees are buzzing and the butterflies are in a flight. We love to see them play, so easy and tender, mild and happy. The fire president walks along an orchard, here and these are best summer fruits, they help for a good inner fire.

One can see almond, walnut and chestnut trees, as well as oaks and oh there are pIneapples growing, and coconuts, also apples and peaches, plums and oranges. We love the citrus fruits says the temple president because they bring good health to our fire. Let's find the best fruits for you and you might take them with you.

The fire president smiles and brings a basket of the best and hand-selected fruits, well ripened and juicy in nature. Life is precious like a wonderful sweet fruit, so full of juice and sept, the fluid that makes us feel alive. Inside on can also find the growth, within fruit that holds seeds, the offsprings for procreation. Nature is beautiful as such fruits grow from alone, just by the power of the sun and rain.

The air friend looks in happiness into the basket and smiles, what a great gift that is but I can not accept, I must be light, for my journey back. No problem, we will send it to you, and we will pack some more for your family. With red cheeks and a grin the walk goes on and the fire and air people are walking towards the procession, that goes on in honour for the daughter of the king.

One can hear loud drums and cymbals, beating in the rhythm of an ancient chant. These hymns are especially designated for the kingdom and the heirs, they shall show the power and grace of the worlds fire. Fire is here to keep and too many have forgotten to make a fire. We here have schools that teach how to make a fire and also how to be good fire bender, because fire is a powerful thing. In the Right hands it can heal and nurture, but wild, it is

unimaginable difficult to handle. That's why we have controlled the fires, yet the children also learn to handle wild fires, which sometimes occur.
Under the guidance of a teacher we can then control and eliminate these.
It is an art, one can learn.

Within the parade there are also young children presenting a wonderful fire show, stunning in nature, fire is a fascinating element isn't it? It dances and flickers, it can be controlled and it can be wild, it can help the world to heal and grow. Wherever there is fire, there are also waters that flow.

There must be water, because without water and air, there is no fire. Yet, there can be light. This is why we also like to meditate with the sunlight, let's go here onto the hill, where we have a glance of the celebration under the setting sun.
The fire and air benders are sitting comfortably for meditation and it happens to be in a serene place, a little

off the stress and noise of the parade, which is in full swing.
The sun sets.

Imagine yourself breathing the sun light. With every breath, there is sun energy streaming into the body and streaming out again. With every inhale we feel the sun light streaming into the body and we feel. After we let go, and the energy from within the body can stream out and be free again. Do this and just see, the wonderful golden light of the sun surrounding your body, as the sun shines from the inside of ones solar plexus, the sun also surrounds us. From within and from outside, there is wonderful, shimmering light. Powerful in nature, yet with the air and with the breath, being still and equal we can be aware of the light.

Sometimes sensations arise, like tickling, vibrating, or throbbing, but that's just the orchestra playing in the distance, we are here and now we are safe and protected with the sun light.

The eternal fire of the sun also shines from within us and we are keepers of this sacred fire, while we smile, the light can come through and come out.
Sometimes one needs a spark, of that joy and happiness and when we see someone smiling it ignites the fire of life, love and laughter.

Let's just laugh together and make our belly bounce, it is very healthy, just like that. HA HA HA, HO HO HO, HI HI HI, HE HE HE, HU HU HU and the belly bounces and we have to hold our belly's so one can feel the belly bounce, again, HA HA HA! HO HO HO! HI HI HI!HE HE HE! HU HU HU! It is not necessary to always have a reason, but laughing and smiling is always healthy in nature, one can relax and let tension dance away.

The serene moment of happiness and laughter remains peaceful and we watch the night come in, the darker the sky gets, the more colourful the sky becomes and eventually the candles

and lanterns are on, enlightening the city.
There is a beautiful process going on at the stream where young students praise the holy river and sway big oil lamps from left and right and into circles. The daughter of the king is very happy and delighted.

We are now safe and sound, in our personal space of light, finding our body and finding our breath, as we equally inhale and exhale the rhythm is smooth and in balance. Our whole body is in balance and we feel the inner flame smoothly burning, within. The stars are sprinkling and the moon shines its cooling light on the earth and into
Our hearts. We are very thankful for our own bodily kingdom and we remain peaceful and equanimous, in harmony and balance.

Let it be light, even in the darkest night.
Rest, Relax and Sleep well.

Salamander Story

<u>1491 words, 20 minutes</u>

Once upon a time there lived a fearless salamander, Salam, who was so fierce Salam could walk through the fire without a problem, actually people who saw it, also say, that Salam was even becoming one with the flame, not even burning or hurt, but totally save.
One with the Fire, yes. And Salam smiles, like nothing happened. It is the nature of a salamander, having practiced life long breathing and meditation, Salam is so relaxed, it just feels warm and comfortable.

One day another Salamander came to Salam to learn, and also this Salamander could do the same. Salam says, practice makes perfect and with the right breathing everyone can love the fire, and live in the fire. Some birds are up in the air, conquering the wind, some fish are under the sea, some animals are living in the soil, and I am nothing special, I am just thankful for the little bit of life.

The Salamander family is very humble and shy. Yet, Salam is out-going and preserves ancient breathing techniques that help one to stay calm in the fire.

Let's come into the place where Salam lives, to have a glance of a true devotee of the flames.

Hello, friend of the fire and curious Traveller! We are here to embrace the breathing and the fire alike, as all fire needs to be maintained with the air, the life force, as I call it. It is the wonderful power within every being. A turtle breathes and breathes very slow, that's why turtles get so old, Salamanders on the other hand breath very intense and quick and therefore we are able to maintain peaceful, in any heated situation.

Also we don't have a heater in our homes, because we are always warm.

Let's come to my favourite place, it is a hill, also called a volcano. But for that we have to step upwards into the hills and up the wonderful and mysterious mountains, Laka, that is the name of the volcano. Laka was here way before anyone else and therefore possesses true knowledge of the air and of course of the inner heat, inside the earth. Inside the earth, there is a core that is so hot, all the masses of rock and metal are fluid, because everything melts together, inside the earth, this core sometimes has an opening, and this opening is sometimes a fountain, a geyser, or a hill, like a volcano.

Let's imagine a wonderful cone-shaped hill, open at the top. There is a huge crater, and inside there is boiling, and cooking hot lava. This stuff is not as small as Grandmas pots, yet it is of the same intensity. The boiling ingredients are just nature's, like the one in Grandmas pot. It is all natural. The Laka Volcano invites us and with the guidance of the Salamander Salam we learn to know about fire and volcanos. This is a steep climb, so one better prepares for the ascension.

Breathe in and out, through the nostrils and the mouth, make the breath audible and listen to the breathing, coming and going, equally in and equally out again. The breathing is coming and going, in and out again. We are now in balance with our goal, we are ascending to the volcano. Breathing and imagining walking over great lava rocks, here and there we have to climb but with the help of Salam we find the right way. It is all for us prepared and one is safe, guided by a trusty friend.

We are breathing and with every breath we can hear the wind blow and the more we ascend, the more intense becomes the breath, in and out, equally in and equally out. The volcano is hot and Laka steams with great respiration. The volcano has been alive more many millions of years and is now ready for us. Are we ready, too?

Let's go and climb higher and higher, with every breath we are getting one step closer to the top. Keep on breathing, and surely we can ask for help, Salam, please, we are almost there Salam answers with hope in the voice. Breathing in and out, just remember always, equal, in and out.

The volcano is there, we are there and now with a last step make it onto the top, looking in the horizon with a smile! Salam is happy for us and we see the giant pot, made by nature. It really is stunning, the lava is golden orange and steams with great intensity. There are many Salamanders around that play hide and seek at the volcano. Yes, this is like a melting pot, says Salam, every Salamander loves to come here. It is like a sacred place for us. The underwater creatures have Neptune's kingdom, the birds have great trees and nests, the earth beings have caves and shelters, and we have Laka.

It is also interesting that the world just grow like this, from the masses of the earth, colliding, and there is the story of a fire king who was so great he stomped into the earth with his Danda, stick, and there we go, there was a hole, which grew to be a volcano, isn't that interesting. Wonderful stories are also around this Salamander who was the priest of the kingdom and brought his family here for a ceremony, and since then we are always celebrating the sunset over here, one can imagine how beautiful the sight is from the volcano over the ocean to the sun.

The world has many great treasure but this here is my favourite one. Now, let's embrace the moment and meditate together. Bring yourself into a comfortable position and don't forget to equally breathe in and out. It is a very easy technique for a cool breath and I always use it when heated up. This can relieve any stress and tension, too.

Let's prepare the position, are you comfortable and breathing, equally in and out? Yes, ok.

There is chance the tongue needs to be prepared because we are now rolling the tongue into the shape of a tube, both sides bending to the top of the base.

The tongue is like a straw and with it we are inhaling and exhaling cool and fresh air. Cool and fresh air is streaming through this tube, into the mouth and one is exhaling with the nose, are you feeling it? Cool and fresh, air breathing into the mouth, with the tongue straw sticking out, and breathing out through the nose. This is a wonderful technique, breathing in, through the mouth, with the tongue rolled inwards and out again, equally in and equally out again.

Wonderful, now let the breathing be normal and just see the sun setting into the ocean, like a great ball of light, going down to rest, tenderly sinking into the bed of the ocean. The Salamanders are chanting nice songs for the sunset:

Oh greatest fire alive, you sun light, so bright!
Let's embrace the change and transform the ways.
From the fire of old and the fine days,
Comes the new and also the night.

Let's celebrate the sight, let's unite within the light,
Let's breathe in harmony and find ourselves in unity.
All beings shall be happy and free, for eternity.
All beings shall be happy and free, for eternity.

This wonderful spectacle is happening everyday, says Salam, yet every time it is special, thank you for being with us and going up this hill of fire, where we Salamanders live. I appreciate and always like to join your way back down, let's ask a friend who is so eager to happily bring us to the home. A winged-Salamander is coming into our sight and Salam says, this is my wife Sally, she likes to bring you home, so you can rest in ease.

Let's embrace a goodbye to Laka and have a nice flight.
While we glide down on Sally's back, we see the ocean reflecting the last sun beams and the sky turning into beautiful colours, on the feet of the hilly land, where Laka resides.
It is a magical place says Sally and I know every time coming here to witness the transformation from day to night is something one-of-a-kind. Like you.
She smiles, we smile back.

Let's all be happy and smile, so all the beings may be in the light, of love, of wisdom, of light. May all the beings Be happy and free. Let's come home for a good nights rest.
We find the breathing again and the awareness travels back into the body. The whole body is fulfilled with a lovely experience from the fire land of the Salamanders, let's remember the best parts and keep surely sharing this story,

into the night. As the light of life shines even in the darkest night.
Sleep well and rest.

Jungle story

Around the Island of the Laka mountains, in the middle of the sea, on a volcano island there is a Jungle with many great trees, long water ways and a happy Jungle kingdom. This kingdom always offers guests to come on a spiritual journey with the guides that are the friendly Ant, Anthony and the great, parrot, Patrick. Anthony and Patrick are a sweet duo, that unlike others never fights. They just laugh, or repeat each other, when there is difficulty understanding. The parrot loves to repeat, loves to repeat and therefore often comes around very funny, very funny. Yet, Anthony is never missing to laugh of his jokes.

Once a parrot was sitting high in the trees and Anthony thought it was Patrick, unaware, that sometimes Patrick's twin is with him. In a matter of a second he awoke and asked, why is this Ant on my nose? Anthony looks at

him, and smiles, may I carry you down the tree? Down the tree? Yes, the sleep got me dreaming of very strong Ants that are able to carry Parrots like me, Parrots like me. Anthony, never ever minded and got his whole Ant family, which are quite a few and there they brought the slumbering Parrot onto the ground. Safely resting in the basin of a paradise island, the Parrot wakes up and is in total wonder, why is my twin making dinner again, was I not suppose to prepare, to prepare? Let's fly to meet my Family, totally still in his dreams Patrick forgot about dinner and starts to cook for the whole family, there comes Anthony and wonders why he is not sleeping in the basin of the Paradise, not sleeping in the basin of the paradise? May I am in disguise?
Let's come here and see, this is where I put thee, I put me?

There comes Patrick's twin ready to cook the dinner and Anthony wonders why he can see, double, any way, what's that for dinner, and what's that for a night? Anthony smiles bright, knowing to invite his whole family. It is time to celebrate and Anthony climbs up the whole tree with his family, we all are ready, is Patrick here, is Patrick here, the twin shows up, yes I am, yes I am, Patrick is Patrick and I am here. Are you all good with rice?

I don't mind, I don't mind. It sometimes all looks the same, as the Ant cannot See, the Parrot left his glasses behind and the whole family of the Jungle was fed that day.

There is a nightly festival, can you hear the drums? We Parrots sing, we Parrots sing and the Ant claps his hands. I know you do. Let's join the festival, let's join the festival. Let invite all the family, all the family. The ants are gathering clapping and chanting the Parrots repeating the phrase.

Let's all be Happy,
Let's all be Happy.

In the World,

In the World,

Of sounds and joy,
Of sounds and joy,

And whenever we can sing,
And whenever we can sing,

One shall let it be,
One shall let it be.

Let's all be friends,
Let's all be friends,

In the World,
In the World,

sounds of happiness,
sounds of happiness,

And whenever we can be,
And whenever we can be,

One shall let it free,
One shall let it free.

Let's all be free,
Let's all be free,

In the World,
In the World,

Sounds of Harmony,
Sounds of Harmony

And whenever we can dance,
And whenever we can dance,

One shall let it be,
One shall let it be.

Let's all be family,
Let's all be family,

In the World,
In the World,

Sounds of unity,
Sounds of unity,

And whenever one can be,
And whenever one can be,

One shall be in harmony,
One shall be in harmony.

The parrot are chanting on and on and it goes on and on, like the Jungle never sleeps, there is always someone awake and singing or chanting, or dancing, or letting it free.
That's the nature of the jungle, Always alive, like the river streams and fountain always springs the jungle always sounds of peaceful harmony.

The trees and animals are all in happiness, dancing and singing, while the sun goes down and there comes the king with a beautiful crown on his head, enjoying the Sunshine and the sounds of peace, harmony and joy. The king is joyful himself and smiles while he waves, decorated with just a loin cloth.
He is very young and the kingdom loves to have a young king, as all the animals follow the guidance of the mountains, where Laka resides. The birds are following the guidance of the trees and

the trees are following the guidance of the earth. The earth is represented by the mountains and the volcano Laka, around the hills, the volcano serves as a playground and for ceremonies as all the jungle inhabitants are coming together to sing and dance.

Life is unique in the Jungle, yet the sunset always comes and never fails, yet today there is a tropical storm which might come down, yet all the people and animals of the jungle are joyfully celebrating and even the jungle storms are splendid showers of warm rain. The wind today is just a little in wonder, it is like searching, where did I leave my keys? The wind is searching for touch and for contact, sometimes some more, sometimes less. This time the Jungle inhabitants love to soothes the storm by singing a heart full song for the storm and for the rain.

Abundant the jungle people show up to soothen the storm with their great instruments - all voices joining together and even the animal king of the jungle, the lion shows up with a furious ROAR. We can join in, opening the mouth and stretching the tongue out: ROAAAR! And again, all together ROAAAAR! The orchestra starts and the lion is in full swing, dancing his most favourite dance. The wind blows but then sees the lion even all the jungle inhabitants just showing up for the celebration, and to soothen the storm.

There comes a white dove and speaks: Yes, the storm comes in peace, bringing us just the finest of the rain, giving us again new water to nurture the plants and trees. To give us a shower, finally! May all be happy!

The storm clouds break and the rain falls in huge drops soothingly onto the heads of all the animals. All the party animals are now very calm and peaceful, just playing their natural songs of happiness and joy.

It rains,

It rains,
The storm is here,
Bring us joy,
And have no fear.

It rains,
It rains,
We celebrate the sight,
Even the sun sets,
Into the night.

Come here,
Come here,
Feel the light,
Breathing in,
And out, alright.

The storm clouds open and the rain tenderly diminishes into a fine sprinkle, whereas the clouds make space for the golden sun setting into the ocean with a surprising last sun beam the sun light and the water of the rain create a sky-full image in all colours.
Can you see the image?

All the colours in the sky,

Oh I wonder why,
We are so blessed,
With such a rain,
Giving us all relief,
From the pain.

Relax the body and prepare for a good and soothing night.
The endless coming and going of the winds is just like the breath, coming in and out, sometimes there might be a cloud, yet the light is always there, shining into the air.
The heaven is open and the breath is free, let it be, let it be,
Let it be,
All beings may live in harmony,
Happily and free,
Like the lion dances for the rain,
The whole jungle enjoys a sight,
Even when the golden sun sets,
Into the good good night,
There might be an image,
Of the whole world in peace,
Find the relaxation and ease.

Relax the body from the crown to the feet and welcome the stars on this beautiful night, there might be, the moon saying hello when the sun lights it face. Let's hope and trust, for our friends and family. Whenever we feel joy, like the whole jungle party in a blissful act, then one might think of the world, and the ones that can receive the joy.

Think of the friends and family and all surrounding you in light, shining even into the fresh and dark night. The jungle party never stops, like the life energy, is always with the breath. This connection ever lasts and helps us through the storm, find comfort even in midst the storm, with the breath, constant and steady.

Find peace within the breathing, because breathing means life, even in the good, good night.
Sleep and rest well.

Monkey story

<u>2006 words, 30 minutes</u>

Once upon a time, there was a monkey living in the Jungle with the name of Cameron and Cameron was a brave and smart Monkey who could climb up the trees to gather bananas and coconuts. The monkey lived well with his family as the jungle provided for everything. All was there for Him and his family.

Jumping left and right and back and forth the monkey had a curious sense of exploring. His mother always says, please be careful, we care about you. The monkey was listening and helped himself to find a comfortable spot in the hammock, where life was just swinging away. Watching the clouds in the sky move and travel, the monkey dreams of foreign lands where his other relatives are living. India, Thailand and Hawaii; all these places have monkeys and Cameron's uncle is just on his way back from India visiting the great city of Agra where the world wonder stands, the Taj Mahal.

Cameron's uncle arrives with a boat and around his neck is hanging a wonderful flower garland, what a surprise, he instantaneously jumps out with a bamboo flute and chants Hare Krishna Hare Krishna, back from India I bring happiness and blessings. He smiles, funny uncle, thinks Cameron and he asks him, please dear uncle can you tell us a story of the great land so far away?

Uncle is charmed and feels obliged to tell a story.
You know, we had a meeting in the great city of Agra and close to it there is the most famous travel destination for Pilgers, people who like to visit holy places, and there the monkeys are very wonderful, dancing and chanting, sitting on the river side and playing with the cows. The cow is also holy and Indians get food to feed the cow, but as soon as we visited, the markets full, the wonders started to happen.

The monkeys in this holy place are serving the best foods, because they are attracting the crowds. Unlike any other animal, here the monkeys dance and put foods on silver plates to bring it to the holy cows and saintly people. There was one older person, a very great personality with a white robe and many flower garlands, there were seven monkeys around him, bringing him this and that.

The monkeys here are wonderful and kind, serving only the freshest ingredients.
The freshest Bananas, one can ever find and what happened with us? We were so welcome, they treated us like a cow! Holy Cow!

The monkey laughs and climbs up a tree. Here, who wants my flower garland? He throws it into the air and Cameron still stunned by the fantastic story catches it. Please uncle, can you tell us another story? He throws the garland back to his uncle. Yes, of course. India is very rich in celebrations and people are singing and drumming on the streets, this is really amazing because it so so loud! But peaceful, there is no one, hurt or sad, everyone is happy and kind.

The fabulous experience of the celebration was a highlight and when one of the monkeys had a flower garland left, he said, maybe you find a dear devotee.
So, I did.

Stories here and there, but everywhere we go we can see how we are all one family. From the ancestors, our fathers the pre-apes, and now us monkeys living a life in paradise.
We are all of one family, and one can see that. Yet, we all like to chant and be happy, and we all like to celebrate with our friends in devotion.
Whatever the reason maybe, we all shall be happy!

I might tell a little more of the monkeys living around the great Palast, the wonder of the world. The Taj Mahal, they are funny but sometimes they are still very wild, playing in the water fountains and jumping into the pools, making each other wet and climbing up the coconut trees, to gather a fresh cool up. It is very warm on the Indian sub continent, but the monkeys don't mind, they are so engaged and happy, they even live in colder climates, up in the hills. We have so many stories to tell, what would you like to know?

How can you not live happily on this island? Uncle smiles and knows Cameron is a sweet heart. It is all possible, I can, but my monkey mind is always moving and I just follow the sense of exploration. I love the sea and there now, it is smart to make my life a living dream.

I know, my father always presented me his stories and always wanted to know, what is it about. He travelled extensively and therefore knew a lot of the world and of the people. Sometimes he even got me a present, a silver banana, I still have this banana, because it reminds me of all the stories. Here in the jungle, we have to live very closely together, I like the freedom like my father.

Freedom? Cameron doesn't know what that is, how can I be free?
Well, one can be free in many ways. Some likes to hang around and enjoy the endless sky, that's freedom. One can also move around freely, like going on a travel.
In between there infinite ways to be free, I'll let you know, maybe you like to sing and play?

Cameron is nodding, yes like everyone. Yes of course. Everyone likes to sing and play. Let's be free with our voice: UH UH UH, the monkey starts to sing:

Free in paradise, what a surprise!
I love the trees and the trees love me,
Free as a monkey.

I love the peace and harmony,
No car,
No house, no spouse, free as a monkey.

Uncle, are you really free? You need a boat, that brings you from one place to another!

Cameron, my dear, because there is the freedom of the wind, the boat can sail, we are just like a guest on board watching the sails set.

What have you seen, dear uncle, is it a good sight?

Cameron, you are my light,
That's why I always come back to home,
Because you are very dear to me.
Let's enjoy the beautiful island harmony.

But will you leave again?

My friend, it is in the space, where the wind blows and where we enjoy a breeze, together with the coming and going of the waves the journey always moves. That's why I am always on the way. Life moves, I move.

You say something with the Monkey Mind, Cameron is a very curious monkey.

Yes, that is within all beings, the humans have it, too. Do you know, when there comes a thought, oh I have an idea, and then somethings let's us let go of this idea and one comes into a dance, maybe I shall go here, or maybe there, or maybe here, the uncle shows with a finger in different directions. It is like you jumping from one tree to another tree. Yes, I am very good at jumping from one tree to another tree, Cameron smiles.

Yes, that's it, let's be happy and do what makes us happy. This is great, uncle, thank you.
Cameron smiles with affection and hops into a tree to find himself a coconut. Uncle looks at him and says, this must be CamConut, you wonderful Cameron, please let's make a song out of that.

Who over got a Coconut, is that You?
Find it Hanging from a tree, is that true?
So many questions and only one answer.
Yes, there is everyone ok, happy and harmony.

What if there is a Coconut, hanging from a tree.
May there be, a wild monkey, climbing up, reaching high,
And once we shake the tree, it falls on the ground, CLAP.
Let's make the sound, and know, why why why.

There is a tree for every fruit. So is everyone one of a kind,
There is a father and mother, even for the monkey mind.
Let's all unite in harmony, and set ourselves free.

Uncle, did you just make up this song?

Well, life is like that, always moving and in flux, spontaneous and new.
And before we knew, there is the chance to redo,

To learn and grow.

Uncle, what is the biggest lesson you have learnt on your travels?

It is the question I ask myself, too. Dear friend and nephew, Cameron, all the lessons are great. Learning to accept myself as a traveller and also accepting my home to always come back.
Let's find ourselves happy and in harmony, playing and the things we live and love.

There is no better and worse, just live a life of love.
Find the playful side of love and devote yourself to that, and when it makes you smile, then everything will be alright.
The monkey smiles and embraces Cameron.

It is nice to have you here with me, dear I am glad to be at home, equally, I am glad to go somewhere.

Remember the meditations I have brought you from Thailand?
Breathing in and equally out, equally in and equally out again.
This is like life, always changing, sometimes we climb up the tree, to fetch a coconut and sometimes one is finding a coconut straight on the ground. Lucky if it has fallen and opened up by itself. May we have a chance to thank our lives and devote our love to the world.

We can breathe and be happy just like that, with all we have, maybe one coconut a day is fine, maybe that's all we need. Maybe we can also live like Hanuman, do you know that the Indian Monkey King is the saviour of a whole kingdom, flying all over the sea to rescue the Queen. I may say that there is the chance to help and enrich the lives of others, this is how my father got this silver banana.

He was a servant of the empire and helped to prepare food, serving a long time and doing the best with his team. Together, the enjoyed also serving the others on big festivals. Because without someone serving, there is no deserving. One has to act according to ones destination and my father was the best server, he got to be honoured with this silver banana, personally from the king.

The king gave this banana to Him and he gave it to me. Isn't that fair, he receives it and presents it to me, now I am serving with this story to help others, like you and maybe when I am old, and cannot travel anymore, you can receive a present like this.

Cameron smiles and instantly thinks, oh now I can climb up this tree to have a banana, but not just for me, but also for my family.
The monkeys brings a whole batch of bananas to the ground, shiny and ripe.

Uncle says, yes, let's go home and bring it together to the family.
This night Cameron learnt to also share his bananas and coconuts, like his uncle is sharing stories, of all kind.

May all beings be kind to one another, may we all share this kindness and give it our friends and family. May all beings be happy, living in Peace, Joy and Harmony.
May, all beings be at peace, living in the happy unity, where no monkey mind springs from left to right, but we serve, as the family is resting, we are now resting, because relaxation and balance are the greatest gift of any being.
See the balance of a tree, a monkey, a bird.
Even sleeping, we can find balance and harmony.
May all beings be happy.
Say good night to the jungle family and have a wonderful rest, bringing a smile to your friends and family, serving with the joy and grace of a smile is always light, even in the darkest night.

Sleep well, and rest.

Rescue story

<u>429 words, 7 minutes</u>

There once was a kingdom in a beautiful land.
Rich and abundant this kingdom had a prince, ready to receive the crown. When he found a wonderful princess, the princess was just the perfect until she disappears. Like a curtain closes, the mystery remains and all the kingdom wonders where she is.

There is also a monkey family who are all watching the woods, and they help to find the coming queen. Like a silver beam a shooting star shot across the realm. The forest lighting up with a bright flash. A shooting star! The help is coming to rescue. The monkeys have a leader, Harmony, who is very wise and genuine. He says, yes I can save the Queen. She send a shooting star to us and we have to find.

She sent a shooting star? Yes, it is her writing and we have to go North to find her. It is the duty of monkeys to serve the kingdom and help with your search.

We can walk to the north to seek out the Queen. The prince is ready to find her and he and the monkey Harmony agree, to be on this mission. Harmony says, you wait here, to stay safe and in peace, prepare the Kingdom for the coming back of the Queen.

Harmony has super powers and flew across the lands to rescue the lady Queen, out of the island, where a coconut tree invited her to come. She was looking for the stars and when she suddenly stood still, she was mysteriously sitting on that tree, in total serenity.

Harmony, waking her up, says I have to rescue you and bring you back to the kingdom it is my duty to serve the prince. The queen smiles and sees the fire of devotion burning with Harmony and together both travel back to the kingdom.

Arriving back, the kingdom was relieved and together they could finally live back in serenity. Together they can enjoy the unity.

Let's imagine sitting under a tree, with nothing to fear, and the wonderful Harmony, coming in great fearlessness and devotion decorated with a silver crown and gems of precious stones hanging from his neck, with strong arms and rings set with Blue sapphires holding a hand to rescue. Everyone who is in fear just scream: HARMONY! And with the help of the greatest devotee of the Kingdom, one shall come to be with you.

Together he gives us the advise to evenly breathe and be balanced, to any surprise, even in the darkest night.
Sleep, rest and relax.

Bird story

<u>448 words, 7 minutes</u>

There once was a forest, a kingdom and a natural reserve, where all the birds came to land and preserve. The birds are on a long journey from the lands far away and coming here everyday, is the sight of the a peaceful place, resting and nesting in this serene sanctuary.
The sanctuary is of a precious golden bird, who delivers messages for the whole country. Faster than any post can, in-time and always secret, this bird is the keeper of many mysteries.

From the beak and around the feather bed there hangs a little letter that flies with the bird to reach its destination. The destination might be far away, yet, the bird brings it anyway and always finds back home. A long, long time, after a journey. The bird rests in the nest and wherever he rests there is always a circle surrounding him with light, asking questions and finding the delight. In his sight, he knows many stories and has visited all the lands, from far to close.

Are we one of those?
Where is the most beautiful place?
How can I deliver on time?

Questions after questions and the golden bird just sings a song, whistling it all night long.

Hear the breath, coming in and going out, the soothing melody of life.
Relax and be content with who you are and you can follow the star. There is the chance, to embrace the timeless now, and one shall ever be ready, to deliver and to be in peace, love and harmony.

The ways of a messenger might be long, but surely bring your favourite song.

I am the light of the world
I am the light of the world
I am the light of the world

You are the light of the world

You are the light of the world
You are the light of the world

We are, We are, We are the light of the world.

Even in this forest and within this kingdom where a bird nests that brings messages to everyone, he always comes back, so a traveller from long, dreamy journeys always comes back, home, into the body with the breath.

Gently breathe in and out again, breathe and feel just fine, and align with the sky, with the sun and the sky, with water, fire and earth. Feel comforted and at peace, one is the light of the world. The world is an endless place of discovery, yet we all come back home.

Enjoy the message of the bird and find the breath, equally and in balance.

May this night be alright and may evenly our light shine into the darkest night, sleep and rest well.

Prince and Princess story

<u>770 words, 10 minutes</u>

There lived a Prince, who is genuine and kind, and he wants to establish a kingdom where all can be kind, so he gives everyone a work, a thing to do, and hence it becomes true, follow this way and once in a life the happiness will be your way.

For every given smile and every breath you do, you might receive the flowers and fruits, for every hand you shake and every present you give, one shall receive the shelter, with the feet one shall walk align and true, now the waters shall be with you.

Find the serenity even in the hardest storms and one shall be relived of any pains. Keep a steady mind and just be kind, just be kind.
The Princess hears him dear, and adds, one shall grow a family tree, of life and love. Having devotion for the here and

the above. Honour the sky and the earth alike, find yourself in peace and relax every night with ease. May we be rewarded with the light of the moon and celebrate together in peace, love and harmony.

The Prince is standing on a pedestal and his Queen is next to Him. He whispers in her ears, without you I am just a normal person, human, like all the same, humble in devotion I became a prince to serve you. To treat the kingdom good for you. The love for the right way of ruling is just for the love of All. He tenderly smiles at her. Both are happy.

The Prince starts to chant a soothing mantra.

You are my moon light, you are the stars that shine bright. You are the one that is next to me, likewise no other can be.
I see in your eyes and tenderly melting is my heart. I am like butter, in the flame of your gaze, melting away. I become soft

and at ease, all the pressure falls off and I can be.

When I look at all we have been through, from the forest, of the kingdoms, living apart, and coming back in serenity. Together we are strong, together we can sing a song.

Of Peace and Love and Unity.
Let's embrace the Harmony,
Prince and Princess on a Pedestal,
Marble and finely carved both stand tall,
Over the endless kingdom's sky
I have the answers why, why, why.
There is love, for one,
There is love for all.

May my love for you equal the love for everyone.
May my devotion to you, equal the devotion for all.
May all my blessings be with you and the world.
May all the grace fulfill the hearts of all.

You are my heart,

So tender and sweet,
You are the symphony,
The wisdom and grace,
Within, I find the space,
When I see your face.
There is this common phrase:
Let there be love,
Let there be light,
Even in the darkest night
May all beings be alright,
In Peace and equanimity,
And whatever may be,
We breathe, we come to thee.

The Prince looks up into the sky, do you ever wonder why we are here, he asks in a child like voice?

The Queen looks at him, as if there is all said, and still a wondrous gaze flashes into the air, while both look up there, comes a shooting star flashing by, like a great wish come true.

Lets find ourselves meditating in the Garden, lush and green. We see the Prince and Princess standing there.

What would you do, which wish shall come true, seeing a shooting star, that could be you. Anything is possible, stay believing and trust the light, even in the darkest night.
Breathe and relax. Let all the stars shine and surround yourself with healing light of love.
Light and Love may shine from our Hearts to the whole world, so all beings shall be at peace. Hold this thought dear and find the smile, always smile, for your friends and family.
Smile in peace, love and unity.

Breathe and know, everything is coming and going, every Kingdom, every prince, every princess all are living a moment, that is special and unique, like every breath is unique, in and out it goes, notice how equal the breath is. Notice how calm and peaceful one can be.

Let it be, in peace, love and unity.

Into the night, sleep, and rest.

Fairytale story

393 words, 6 minutes

There once was a curious traveller, going from place to place, always in wonder, where is the magic, where does the story come true, where is the me and where is you?

There came a man, so humble and kind, with wisdom so long like his ears and his gaze was straight into ones eyes. Well, you search, and still search? Become the stillness and let search find you. Let it be.
The fairy tale is coming to you, just sit still.

The traveler stands still in awe and sits down, without a tone. His eyes are almost falling and as they are half closed he wakes up by a flash, in front of his eyes it must have a fairy. He gazes onto the nose, yes indeed! A fairy waves at me!

Welcome, you, met our Teacher who loves to fulfill the search and as you have been searching until here, you shall see, what a fairy world looks like. Wait here and close your eyes. Fully and Gently.

Let's be prepared, here comes the ferry dust.
Like flower petals so kind and soft falling unto the skin,
The ferry dust comes from the fairy world within,
In a sparkling source we can finally see,
There is more, so let it be,

Coming to the world of a wonderful possibility.
There sits the teacher in a shiny glow,
To the feet of a tree, and a flower to show.
Everything may be, and we can ask the wise,
What life may be, may be?
Will I be free, is there eternity?

The wise one with the gaze opening hearts, tenderly speaks from the heart.

All is One, of a kind, in a rhyme, even in the sunshine, like this flower here, we can blossom and listen and feel. The flower rose and stands from alone, growing to be a wonderful hedge, I am the flower without a thorn, life is peaceful and we shall be born, every moment, breathing, fleeting like my scent, there is the sky the heavens tent.
Just lay there in wonder and let it be, it will come to thee.

The wise one, and the ferry and the flower wave for a good night and we shall find, all light, even in the darkest night.

May all beings be happy and free.
Light is eternity.

Sleep well.

www.ingramcontent.com/pod-product-compliance
Lightning Source LLC
Chambersburg PA
CBHW071810080526
44589CB00012B/740